Randy, a fireman, was called in for a four-alarmer. He raced to his car, jumped in and turned the key in the ignition. Then he heard a voice say, "Stop!"

He looked around. There was no one there. Then he heard it again. "Get out of the car."

Randy pushed open the door and walked to the rear of the car. And stopped, stunned. Little Marie Puckett was sitting on the ground, her back resting against his back bumper, happily playing with a shovel as she was digging dirt and scooping it into a small bucket. "Hi, Uncle Randy," she said.

He hadn't heard her playing behind his car. He had been about to back the car out of the driveway, when—*he heard a voice that spoke to him as clearly as anyone ever had . . . but there was no one there!*

Other Avon Books by
Don Fearheiley

MIRACLES

ANGELS AMONG US

DON FEARHEILEY

AVON BOOKS

An Imprint of HarperCollinsPublishers

AVON BOOKS
An Imprint of HarperCollins*Publishers*
10 East 53rd Street
New York, New York 10022-5299

Copyright © 1993 by Don Fearheiley
Published by arrangement with the author
Library of Congress Catalog Card Number: 93-90342
ISBN: 0-380-77377-5
www.avonbooks.com

First Avon Books Printing: November 1993

Avon Trademark Reg. U.S. Pat. Off. and in Other Countries, Marca
Registrada, Hecho en U.S.A.
HarperCollins® is a trademark of HarperCollins Publishers Inc.

Printed in the U.S.A.

30 29 28 27 26 25 24 23

Dedicated

to

TEENIE

Who taught me the most about angels

Contents

Contents

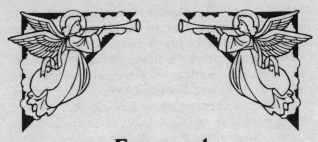

Foreword

Everyone knows about angels, at least at the level of sentiment. Greeting cards, songs, and poems portray the goodness, purity, and love inherent in an angel, applying these qualities to sweetheart or spouse.

But are angels real?

For most people this question revolves around how they view the Bible. The Bible says that Abraham, Jacob, Moses, Joshua, Gideon, David, Elijah, Zacariah, Joseph, Mary, and Peter all saw angels. Three angels were actually mentioned by name—Michael, Gabriel, and Raphael. Michael was mentioned in three books: in Daniel he is described as the great prince charged to defend the people of God; in Jude he is seen as the archangel fighting with Satan over the body of Moses; and in Revelation he is shown leading his angels against the dragon. Tradition has Gabriel presiding over paradise, and according to Mohammed, Gabriel was the angel who at God's command dictated the Koran. Raphael is considered the guardian angel of science and knowledge, the healer of disease.

Passing time built the traditions of other angels.

Medievel Jewish scholars declared there were 301,655,722 angels. Gustav Davidson took a more limited approach in his *A Dictionary of Angels*. Drawing names from the Bible, rabbinical and cabalistic literature, writings of the church fathers, and poetry, he fashioned brief biographies of 3,406 angels. Some of these angels had an elevated purpose, like Uriel, archangel of salvation, often credited with warning Noah of the flood. But other angels liked to play pranks, as did Baltazard.

No one knew how angels looked, but by the fourth century A.D. artists conceived them with wings. Were they male or female? Another heated question. But in A.D. 1272 Thomas Aquinas reasoned that angels could assume whatever aspect they desired, and were therefore neither male nor female. Luther and Calvin both believed in angels, but Luther prayed that God would not allow angels to enter his dreams, for they were distracting to his work.

Then in the post-Darwinian nineteenth century angels lost their hold on the public imagination. Science, reason, and belief in natural progress were the panaceas of the day. Anyone who saw an angel in this kind of world was considered mentally deranged.

Today, however, people know that science and reason alone do not give the whole truth of existence. Science can be used to destroy the world as well as help it materially progress. And many people believe, along with Billy Graham, that angels are "incorporated spirits created by God to worship him and carry out his will."

Yet angels remain a mystery, and in the Bible mystery is added to mystery. For angels came suddenly without warning, serving different purposes. They could be seen as shining lights or as ordinary mortals. Their appearances were fleeting. Obviously they came from another realm of existence—not separated from mortals by light-years but by a different dimension of being. If they came, and if they still come, they somehow pierce the fabric of our world from outside.

In this book are stories about angel visits. The names and places have been changed, but the visits are based on actual reports as described in print and on television. Those who tell firsthand, direct, and personal accounts of angel visits do so with absolute conviction that supernatural intervention has taken place. They would tell you—regardless of how impossible or improbable the event seems—that something real affected them. We make no such claim for the events in this book. These stories are a form of our reporting to you the kinds and types of angel visits that people have testified really happened. You, the reader, will make your own interpretation. We are happy to present these stories for your entertainment, and if you choose, for your enlightenment.

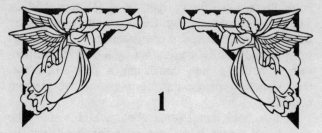

1

Warren's Angel

The angels are near to us, to those creatures by God's command they are to preserve

—LUTHER

He was putting the final touches on Spaggie when his boss called him on the intercom.

"Warren, you about finished with the drawing?"

"Almost, R. B." Spaggie was smiling up at him from the art board. Warren hoped R. B. would be equally sanguine about the situation. He picked up the art board, smiled back at Spaggie, and then left his office.

He passed by two other offices on the way to see R. B., both of which contained artists working industriously over angled drawing desks. The wall of the hallway was gray fabric exhibiting numerous samples of art that represented past prize-winning advertising campaigns. Lucas Communications, Ltd. every year accumulated a few Diamond Awards in categories of print ads, folders/flyers, radio commercials, direct mail campaigns, television spots. R. B. was always tense this time of year when every local advertising agency submitted entries considered its best work of the past twelve months. Winning awards in any category made R. B. happy, but winning "Overall Best Campaign" made him the happiest.

"An award represents future business," R. B. liked to say. And that was really the crux of it. Maybe awards massaged the egos of most winners, but for R. B., winning meant bucks—future bucks. Awards built a reputation which attracted new clients and kept current clients coming back.

"An agency lives off its reputation," was another R. B. dictum, and certainly Lucas Communications had a reputation for being one of the city's most creative houses.

Warren Young had been with the agency for eight years. Fresh out of art school, he had started as a draftsman. In two years he was promoted to Artist B, two more years to Artist A, and Master Artist the year after that. But R. B. kept a close eye on all his talent, and he discerned that Warren's personality fitted him for an even bigger job.

Actually, R. B. didn't come up with the original idea. Warren was working with Abner Kelly on the Farm Fresh Dairy account. Abner was the agency account exec assigned to Farm Fresh. Usually Abner was very friendly, able to schmooze clients with the best of them. But for some reason the president of Farm Fresh did not like Abner (Warren thought it stemmed from a time when Abner started to light up a cigarette in the president's office without the president's permission), and after many hours consultation the president suddenly threw out all the work done up to that point. Abner committed the unpardonable sin—he blew up in the client's face. Lucas Communications was about to lose Farm Fresh, so R. B. blew up in Abner's face. At which time R. B. pointed a finger at Warren and said since he was the artist, he should come up with new ideas and sketches and get back with the president and save the account.

Warren did save the account, justifying R. B.'s faith, and was launched as an account exec. But he was an account exec with a difference. R. B. did not want to lose his art talent, nor did Warren want to quit drawing, so he was a combination exec/artist—unique at the agency—and for the next year was R. B.'s "Number One Son."

But that was two years ago. When the economy went south, so did some of Lucas's clients. R. B. cut back on artists and copywriters—keeping the bottom line securely in the black. He even cut one account exec, Bill Ridley, who was old enough to get social security along with his pension. But rumors were that others might be cut.

Warren was walking through the office pool area when a voice to his rear arrested him.

"Warren—" a voice so musical it sang. Warren turned.

"Hello, Hazel," he said. Hazel McIntyre approached rapidly, holding an art board.

"Does this look all right?" she asked.

He looked at the drawing, a proposed logo for a startup company that produced music videos. "A beautiful job," he said. Beautiful, right—but the real beauty was standing before him.

Hazel had been working only four months, coming from an art school in Atlanta. Her hair was dark red with fiery highlights, her skin milk-pale. Green was her favorite color, which was good because her eyes were green, with the longest lashes he had ever seen. During her first day on the job most of the guys had trouble not staring. They still did.

She constantly experimented with her hair—it was long enough to give her a new look every day, from loose natural waves to ponytail to bangs to a mixture of this and that. Combined with her taste in clothes, the total effect was always stunning.

He sighed. She was twenty-three, making him feel old at thirty-two.

"Do you think Mr. Bonnell will like it?"

Jed Bonnell was the account exec on her job, and his best friend. "I can't speak for Jed," he said, "but this is good." Actually, no one could speak for Jed, a sixteen-year veteran in the advertising game. He spoke for himself. He had worked for five different agencies in his career, not because he wasn't talented, but because of his frank, some would say abrasive, personality. Not all clients responded to his honest, plain-speaking approach, but the ones who did stayed with him in agency moves. That's why he kept being hired by new agencies after loosing favor with his old boss.

Warren wasn't sure why Hazel seemed to have elected Warren as a father figure. He really felt too young to be anyone's mentor. But from day one she had given him that special smile that singed his hair follicles. He had lots of hair—black—but his nose was too big and his neck too thin and he wore dark-rimmed glasses. "Nerd" was a fighting word, and a few guys in art school and beyond had learned the hard way that a circumspect tongue meant never having to say "I'm sorry."

What was really rough on him was having to ignore the little hints of availability she kept pressing upon him. There was a time when he would gladly have leaped over his desk to earn one little sign of her favor. But for four months he had acted friendly, professional, and—stupid. That's what Jed had called him.

"Plain stupid," he said. "Every single guy in this firm—and probably a few married ones—has made a pitch for her. She's as cold as a roofless igloo in a snowstorm."

Warren groaned. "Roofless igloo?"

"You know what I mean," Jed said. "Or maybe you don't, because she doesn't seem cold with you. Everybody's buzzing. Do something!"

"I have a girlfriend," Warren said.

"I'm not knocking Pauline. But a divorcée with a five-year-old kid? Compared to Hazel? Get real."

"It wouldn't feel right."

Jed shook his head. "Are you engaged to Pauline?"

"No."

"Going steady?"

"Not really."

"What kind of commitment is that? You're free as a buzzard going after a road kill."

Warren groaned again. "Will you forget the similes? Please!"

"I'm telling you, that girl has her eyes glued to you."

"And why is that?" Warren asked. "Why me?"

Jed grinned quizzically at him. "I don't know. Maybe she feels sorry for you. Maybe you remind her of a dead uncle she idolized as a kid. Or maybe, just maybe, she sees a decent guy who's brighter than he is handsome, who's talented in her own field, and who laughs at jokes and sometimes even says something funny himself. Or maybe—" Jed's grin was wider, "she's just crazy."

Now Hazel looked at Warren as though the king had just bestowed knighthood. She left with a final smile that almost made him forget where he was going.

R. B.'s office was dubbed Fern Valley by the patrons of the lower order. R. B.'s wife was a potted plant freak, a slightly overweight and fast-talking woman in her mid-forties who delighted in personally supervising the look and feel of her husband's working environment. Hanging ferns combined with potted plants to create an atmosphere of outdoor claustrophobia.

"Sit down, Warren, my boy." R. B. was standing and gesturing Warren to a chair. As Warren sat, R. B. moved around his desk to a nearby chair so that the desk would not be between them. Warren was already mentally ducking his head. When R. B. went into his overly friendly routine you knew something else was about to come down. Like maybe an ax?

"Let me see the drawing," he said. Warren handed it to him, and R. B. looked intently at it, his face impassive. Then he looked admiringly at Warren.

"Not bad. Not bad at all," he said. "You think Salisbury will like it?"

"I hope so," Warren said. Marcus Salisbury was president of the Spaghetti Spot franchise chain.

"Great idea you had about trying to humanize the concept of spaghetti. Great idea!"

Now Warren inwardly began to hunker down

more, waiting for whatever was coming. Spaghetti
Spot was in trouble. Marcus Salisbury, a billionaire
who had made his early money in oil, started the
Spaghetti Spot chain with fanfare and trumpets—
emphasizing that people could now find welcome relief from the usual litany of burger, fish, and chicken
restaurants. Spaghetti—the universally loved food—
was now available with fast-food convenience and
low price. This special spaghetti was, of course, developed by Salisbury's great-grandmother, who
brought the recipe for the sauce with her from Italy
when she emigrated to America. It has remained a
closely guarded secret ever since.

But after two years of rapid expansion in the
Southeast, business was on a downward trend. At
first the thought was that all restaurants were
slumping because of economic conditions. But recent
figures showed that the fast-food business was now
moving upward again. Spaghetti Spot—still down.

If all else fails, think advertising.

Lucas Communications earlier had placed a little
local advertising for the five outlets in the city. But
now R. B. felt the time was ripe to make a pitch for
regional advertising. He proposed to the home headquarters of Spaghetti Spot that Lucas develop ideas
for an entirely new regional campaign that would attract more customers. Reaching agreement to develop
a pilot project, R. B. had given the assignment to
Warren.

As Warren considered Spaghetti, he could see an
immediate handicap for the drive-in business that had
become so big in the burger fast-food outlets. Spaghetti was more messy. Spaghetti could be spilled on

clothes in moving vehicles. For spaghetti, most people would want to go inside.

This meant larger facilities than was needed for the burger, chicken, and fish places. Unfortunately, many of the Spaghetti Spot franchises had limited space. How to entice more customers utilizing current space?

People would still drive through for spaghetti to take home. And if more people wanted to eat inside the restaurant, local owners would be encouraged to expand their facilities.

So ignore the mess factor and concentrate on making people think spaghetti. What is appealing about spaghetti? It tastes good, right. But, spaghetti is so— spaghetti. Where is its personality?

Warren's mind then jumped to the most appealing personality of his childhood—Puff the Magic Dragon. What about a dragon? Not a scary dragon, but a friendly dragon that kids would love? Like Casper, the Friendly Ghost? What if he could create a small, friendly, green dragon who liked spaghetti? And his name—Spaggie. Spaggie—smiling, happy Spaggie—on every bib given to customers, on every poster, in hand-out comic books featuring his adventures in Spaghetti Land?

Humanizing spaghetti—with an adorable dragon. Hook the kids—hook their parents.

R. B. liked the idea. Warren developed sketches, rendered drawings. The drawing he had with him now represented the latest revision for presentation to Marcus Salisbury himself. After this would come drawings of different poses to illustrate what could be done in various advertising and promotional approaches.

"I'm proud of you, my boy," R. B. said. "If Salisbury buys this, we can take over the regional advertising for Spaghetti Spot, and as they expand we can go with them. We could someday have a national account."

Warren could almost see the dollar signs dancing in front of R. B.'s eyes. "I hope so," he said.

R. B.'s expression changed. "And we need an account like Spaghetti Spot," he said. "I haven't told anyone this, but we've lost the Beacon Motel and Jeffrey's Food accounts. I'm having to let Cassidy and Peters go."

Warren didn't know what to say. Cassidy had been here longer than he, while Peters was relatively new. "Everyone has to pull his own weight," R. B. went on. "You've got to be able to sell and deliver in this business. Fail at either one—" R. B. gave a little shrug.

Warren thought of Jed, who had brought four accounts with him to this firm. Jed's position was secure as long as he had those accounts in his pocket. Or until—Warren smiled to himself—R. B. caught him spitting into one of his wife's ferns.

But then R. B. was looking seriously at him. "Warren," he said, "I value your ability highly—"

Here it comes, Warren thought.

"—very highly. You rose from the ranks, not that I hold artists of less worth than account executives. But you've shown yourself unusually creative, and despite the fact you haven't been able to bring in a lot of new accounts the past couple of years, I was glad to have you on board."

Now it comes, Warren thought.

"Tough times," R. B. said, "troubling times. But

this Spaghetti Spot account could make a difference for us. Do you understand what I'm saying?"

"I think so."

"I don't want to let anyone else go. But I can't overstress how important it is that we sell Spaggie to Salisbury. We need the Spaghetti Spot account." R. B. smiled. "Then I think I could safely say there is no danger anyone else will have to go. At least for awhile. A lot depends on you, my boy."

As Warren left the office one thought was blinking like a neon sign. Spaghetti Spot or I'm history.

Back in his office he looked at his drawing. Not exactly a work of art, but it communicates. Communicates what? Joy of youth? Dreams of childhood? Hunger for spaghetti? Do I really care what one guy in a fast-food company thinks of a little green dragon with a hooked tail?

He thought of the comic strip he had been working on at home in his spare time. He hoped one day to sell it to a syndicator. Then he could quit worrying about selling spaghetti or soap or stain-resistant carpet and start worrying about just being funny. Of course, advertising was really the funniest business on earth. The trouble was, account execs had to treat it like it was a serious business.

As he stared at Spaggie's smiling face an idea began to take shape. He reached for a pencil and tracing paper. He visualized the face of Marcus Salisbury, and began to draw. Soon another Spaggie began to take shape, but with a difference. As Warren worked, a faint resemblance to Salisbury emerged through Spaggie's familiar features. He went to his drawing board then, and began to trace the outline on an art board. Then he inked and finally colored until a finished drawing lay alongside his original drawing. Two Spaggies, but ah, yes—the second was the better.

It might work. Perhaps Salisbury would be flattered by the resemblance, even appreciate the fact that he personally, in a unique way, would be touching the lives of the three- to eight-year-olds who would adopt Spaggie as their own. On the other hand, Salisbury might hate the idea and think it insulting, forever shutting the door on Lucas Communications' ever working for them again.

Should he show the new drawing to R. B.? Warren grinned to himself. Nah—R. B. had made it clear that the challenge was his. He could bring home the bacon or find another pig to barbecue. Whatever he decided to do would be his decision alone. Besides, this decision might end up being the last fun he'd have at Lucas Communications.

The phone jarred his thoughts. He recognized the voice.

"Pauline? What's wrong?"

She was agitated. "Can we meet for lunch?"

"Sure. But what's the matter?"

"I'll talk to you then," she said. "Eleven-thirty at Carrolton's?"

"See you there," he said, hanging up. Two years earlier Pauline Craig divorced Darrell Craig, an ophthalmologist in the Baptist Hospital Medical Building who specialized in cataract operations. They had a neat five-year-old daughter named Jennie, whom Warren adored. The fact that Pauline was a great-looking blond didn't dampen Warren's interest in her. But the fact that Jennie was her daughter was an even stronger selling point.

As for Darrell Craig, Warren had met and liked

him. One night he was probing to see what had gone wrong between Pauline and Darrell.

"I know he's an ophthalmologist, but what did you see in him?" he asked. "Why did you set your sights on an ophthalmologist?" He had thought he was being witty, but he didn't get an appreciative reaction from Pauline. In fact, that was one of the few reservations he had about Pauline—she seldom laughed. Not at his jokes. He had always like girls with a sense of humor. But—Jennie was her daughter, and Jennie laughed.

He hated to think it, but his other reservation was her church involvement. She was a little extreme in that part of her life. Pretty conservative, in fact, about the Bible, believing in miracles and angels and Old Testament examples of God's wrath that were hard to swallow. He had nothing against church. As a kid he had gone to church all the time. But he had outgrown it, and Pauline was always asking him to attend with her. In fact, she probably had plenty of reservations about him. But something else about him must be keeping her interested.

Pauline wasn't bitter toward Darrell. He hadn't been playing around. The problem was somewhat the opposite. As Pauline had tried to explain it in a kind way, she felt his romantic proclivities were deficient. The divorce had been her idea, but it hadn't been an easy decision. She had prayed about it, and even with the Bible's strict admonitions against divorce, she felt that God was leading her in that direction.

The divorce was amicable, and Darrell agreed to terms for alimony and child support that were more than adequate. Pauline resumed her career as a dental assistant, which was how Warren had met her. His dentist, Dr. Cooper, had introduced them during Warren's annual checkup.

Carrolton's was an Italian garden-style restaurant which featured pasta and a great salad. Pauline was waiting in the foyer, wearing a three-quarter length light tan wool coat over her white uniform. As they followed the hostess to a table he saw spaghetti in booth after booth. Spaggie, you have your work cut out for you, Warren thought.

They both ordered salad and iced tea. "Something happened this morning," Pauline said. Warren could tell she was still agitated. "Jennie almost got killed."

He grabbed her hand. "Is she all right?"

She nodded. "Yes. But she almost was run over."

"How did it happen?" he asked.

"In the parking lot at school." Pauline dropped Jennie off at the Montessori school every morning on her way to the dentist's office. "I didn't just let her out because I wanted to talk to the teacher. We had to park a long way from the door. We got out of the car and Jennie saw a friend and began running. She ran right behind another parked car that suddenly backed out real fast. The driver didn't see her."

She stopped talking and Warren waited. Finally he said, "She didn't get hit?"

"No."

"Well, maybe she learned a lesson," he said, relief in his voice.

"Warren," Pauline's voice trembled. "The car would have hit Jennie."

"But you said it didn't. The driver saw her in time."

"It didn't hit her because someone stopped the car."

"That's what brakes are for."

"Someone outside the car stopped it," she said. "Someone jumped in front of Jennie and the car hit him and stopped dead."

Warren stared at her. "Who was he?"

Pauline couldn't keep her voice from trembling. "No one saw him but me. He disappeared before I got to Jennie."

"You mean someone only you could see kept the car from hitting Jennie?"

She nodded.

If Pauline had a sense of humor, Warren would have laughed. But he knew Pauline was not laughing, so he said nothing. The car didn't hit Jennie—sure. But a car stops when the driver's foot stomps on the brake. Jennie had been lucky.

Then Pauline said in a low voice, "I think it was Jennie's guardian angel."

Warren didn't know what to say. Pauline was serious. Not the time for him to be witty. She's really into this, he thought. The Bible talked about angels, sure. But now she was imagining she saw one in the 1990s.

That afternoon he did some more work with Spaggie. He was going with the Salisbury resemblance. He had two more days to tie it all together— proposal with budget estimates for an intense local media saturation conducted over a limited time frame to be followed by evaluation to determine what worked best and what didn't. If the pilot project were successful, then any needed revisions could be made before a regional breakout. Spaggie would become the symbol for every Spagetti Spot in the Southeast.

If—Marcus Salisbury bought the proposal.

At four o'clock he stepped out of his office and headed for the break room. He wanted a cup of coffee. Hazel was sitting at a table, drinking a Tab. He poured his coffee, hesitated, then sat in a chair across the table from her. She smiled at him, and he sipped his coffee, staring at her. She was really something to look at. Then his mouth surprised him.

"Will you have dinner with me tonight?" he asked. He couldn't believe it. He hadn't meant to ask her that. Anyway, he would never ask any woman for a dinner date at the last minute. He deserved to be turned down flat.

Instead, she looked at him for a long moment and then asked, "Are you sure?"

"Yes," he said, suddenly hopeful.

"Why?"

"I've thought about asking you for a long time."

"But why tonight?"

Pauline's face briefly flashed through his mind, and he found himself saying, "Maybe I wanted to see if you have a sense of humor."

She looked puzzled.

"Look," he said, "let's try it another time. I'll give you more notice."

"OK," she said. He smiled and started to get up.

"What time?" she asked.

"What's that? Oh—well, how about Friday?"

"I meant what time tonight."

"Tonight?"

"I said OK, I'd have dinner with you tonight." She was grinning. "You have trouble communicating, don't you, Mr. Young."

"How about eight," he said, "and please don't call me Mr. Young."

"I'm in the Rayburn Apartments. You know where that is?"

He nodded, "Second Avenue, North—on the Riverfront?"

"You can park in back. Just buzz, I'll let you in."

All of a sudden he felt better than he had for a long time. He might find out a number of other things about her tonight, but he already knew she had a sense of humor.

Second Avenue on the Riverfront was a series of restored buildings originally constructed in the nineteenth and early twentieth centuries. Commercial life in the city had once focused on river traffic. After decades of gradual deterioration, the downtown area underwent a renewal—supported by local tax dollars and early risk takers. New businesses opened up in buildings restored to their early grandeur. A Riverside Park was developed, and new apartments appealed to those who wanted to live at the cutting edge of the latest housing trend. A vital part of the new establishments were varied restaurants catering to fish lovers, steak lovers, pasta lovers, and odd-food lovers.

As Warren pulled into the parking lot behind Rayburn Apartments he realized he was hungry for some lemon sole, a speciality of Cutter's Cuisine, three blocks away on Second Avenue overlooking the river.

He was buzzed in, took the elevator to the third floor, and stopped at Apartment D. He knocked on the door, and when the door opened he stopped breathing.

Hazel had freed her hair, which flowed loosely around her head in lustrous red natural waves. She wore a green knit dress that closely hugged every

curve of her body. Around her neck was a one-strand
gold necklace that tried to call his attention away
from what was below it to the beautiful neck and face
above it. He knew his mouth was open and he closed
it abruptly.

She smiled and he knew, somehow, that his destiny
was fixed. And he didn't mind at all.

She suggested they walk to Cutter's. Street parking
and a few crowded pay lots were the only parking
available in this section of restored buildings. A lot
of people were on the street, and Warren enjoyed
checking out the variety of shops available to the
walk-in traffic.

At Cutter's they were seated by a large window
facing the river. A steamboat was docked not far
away, and Warren could see tourists walking the
gangplank to get on board.

The dinner was perfect, the fish was perfect, the
service was perfect, the conversation was perfect, and
if Warren learned anything, it was that he had been a
fool not to have tried to date this woman months ago.
He thought of Jennie, and for a moment was lost in
the thought that someday he and Hazel might have
their own Jennie.

"What are you thinking?" her voice jarred him. He
blushed, and as she watched him stammer out some
kind of answer she had a premonition—perhaps the
kind of insight that only comes from some ancient
wisdom of womankind—that this man would be special to her. This man could blush—she filed that
knowledge in her secret heart of hearts.

They stayed at the table for more than two hours,
each talking and sharing in building a bond made
stronger by learning something of each other's his-

tory, concerns, and ambitions. Warren left a larger than usual tip when they left.

Outside the sidewalk was largely deserted. Few people were walking; street traffic had died down. Warren had a sudden sharp doubt, a wariness about safety. Now he wished they had a car parked nearby. As they walked slowly he quieted his inner emotion. The old reputation of downtown no longer applied. There were more streetlights now, and renewal had driven out the winos and muggers and street people.

She was holding his arm and he was talking about Spaggie and the state of his proposal for his meeting with Salisbury. He did not relate his feeling about the importance of that meeting to his future at Lucas Communications. On this night he did not want her to sense any concern on his part about what might happen. And that meant on this walk, too. Because he still felt uneasy.

There was nothing he could see that should worry him. They were only two blocks from her apartment. An occasional car would pass them. The street was lighted well. But the feeling persisted.

Halfway down the block was a narrow alley that ran between Second Avenue and First Avenue. As they walked closer they saw a man suddenly appear out of the alley and stop, leaning against the corner of a building and facing them. The man stayed motionless, staring at them, and Warren felt his neck hair stiffen and tingle.

They kept walking toward the man, and Warren held tighter to Hazel's hand, trying to reassure her. The man had a right to be there, but Warren didn't like the way he was staring. And the tension in the pit of his stomach heightened the closer they came.

Warren could feel his muscles hardening as he antic-ipated something unpleasant. Would there be a knife? A gun? A mugging? Warren was ready for anything. He felt a kind of rage building. No one was going to threaten this woman beside him. He was prepared to lash out, kick, strike in any manner necessary, and there would be no mercy.

Now they were ten feet away and closing. The man kept staring. Coming abreast of him Warren was ready for anything. But then they were past. Warren glanced backward. The man was still staring but not moving. Warren led Hazel in walking faster.

Finally he said, "Did you sense any danger with that guy?"

"Yes," she said, "but somehow I wasn't worried." Her answer lightened his mood.

At her door he used her key to unlock it. She smiled up at him, "I had a wonderful time."

He wanted to say something eternally memorable. But all he could think of to say was, "Me, too." Then he said, "I want us to—" His voice died out.

She kept that wonderful smile on her face and softly said, "I know."

"Dinner Friday night?" he asked. She nodded, and he started to turn away. She grabbed his arm.

"Just a moment," she said, and hooked her other hand around his neck. She pulled his head down and her lips gave him the greatest charge of electricity since Benjamin Franklin flew the kite.

The next morning he woke up wanting to sing. He did. Then he whistled, feeling like he was floating in the upper levels of giddiness. Whistling while he shaved wasn't his all-time best idea. Toilet tissue stemmed the cut. Orange juice and bacon and eggs.

He cooked his own breakfast—he must be feeling good!

Then a quick look at the local news before heading for work, and Hazel.

One story caught his attention. A mugging was reported on Second Avenue last night, near the Rayburn Apartments. A couple was accosted near an alley at around 11:15. The man was shot and in serious condition at St. Mary's Hospital, while his wife suffered a head injury but was later released. A suspect was later arrested.

Warren immediately called the police station. After explaining that he had seen a man loitering near an alley in that area last night, the sergeant asked him to come in.

Calling the office and saying he'd be late, he went to the station and was introduced to Sergeant O'Malley. After hearing Warren's story, Sergeant O'Malley nodded.

"I appreciate your coming in," he said, and went to a filing cabinet and took a bound compilation of many sheets from the top. He turned the sheets until he found what he was looking for. He showed the sheet to Warren. The sheet contained front and side pictures of four men. The sergeant pointed to one.

"Is this the guy you saw?"

Warren recognized him. He was thinner, but no question. "That's him," he said.

"We got a make on him from Mrs. Patterson, the wife of the shooting victim. You know, she was lucky he didn't shoot her instead of hitting her on the head. You never can figure guys like Nick Pillow."

"Is that his name?" Warren asked.

"Right. He's already served two sentences. Three

strikes and you're out—he'll be out of circulation for a long time."

"I had a feeling about him," Warren said, "the way he stared at us. We walked right by him. I thought sure he was going to do something, but he just let us go by."

"You were luckier than the Pattersons."

Warren hesitated. "Sergeant, this may sound silly to you, but could I see him?"

The sergeant looked at him strangely. "Why?"

"The guy obviously wanted to rob someone. I'd like to know why he let us pass him. Why did he pick on the Pattersons instead of us?"

The sergeant smiled. "Maybe you had a guardian angel."

"I'm serious, Sergeant."

The sergeant shrugged. "OK. Why not? But he probably won't talk to you."

"I'd like to try."

The sergeant led him through a series of doors that were opened electronically by guards who pressed buttons. Then the sergeant led him into a passageway between cells on either side, finally stopping near the end.

"Hey, Pillow," the sergeant yelled, "someone wants to talk to you."

Nick Pillow was lying on his cot, his arm thrown over his face. His voice came muffled, "I got no one to talk to."

"Get over here!" the sergeant said. Nick lowered his arm from his face and looked blearily toward them.

"Go away," he said.

"I just want to ask you a question," Warren said.

Nick slowly sat up, then rose unsteadily and slowly crossed to the bars. "What do you want?"

"You remember me?" Warren asked.

Nick squinted his eyes. "No."

"Last night. Near the alley. I walked right into you."

Nick squinted again. "You with that gorgeous red-headed broad?"

"You do remember," Warren said.

"Yeah, I remember."

"You let us go by. I wondered why."

"You ought to know," Nick said.

"No, really. I'm curious. Why did you let us go by?"

Nick shook his head back and forth. "I'm not stupid. I was a little strung out last night, but I'm not crazy!"

"What are you talking about?"

"That guy coming up behind you was mean looking, man. He was staring straight at me and he had his hand in his pocket like he was carrying a piece. I wasn't going to do anything with him back there."

Warren looked at the sergeant, who had a questioning look on his face. He looked back at Nick and said, "Thanks." Then he motioned to the sergeant and they went back through the passageway.

Back at the front desk Warren turned to the sergeant. "Sergeant, there was no one walking behind us last night."

"He sure saw someone."

"But there was no one there."

The sergeant stared at him. "You know, I made that crack about your guardian angel. Now I'm not laughing."

2

Gale's Angel

*And we cried to the Lord for help. He listened to
us and sent an angel*

—NUMBERS 20:16

Gale Hunter felt good about being sixteen. She had
her own driver's license. Hurrah! But actually she
wasn't that interested in having her own car yet, not
when she could ride on her Honda Shadow VT-600
teal and black motorcycle. Her mother got really mad
at her father when he bought the bike for her on her
birthday. She had heard them arguing one night, so
she knew she was going to get the bike. She decided
then that she would make it easier on her mother—
she'd settle for a sedate color. Teal and black were
sedate enough for anyone.

But, somehow, the color scheme didn't seem to
make Mother appreciate the bike's beauty, so maybe
she should have gone for red. Dad wouldn't have
minded, that's for sure.

He had his own bike—a Honda Shadow VT-1100,
a kind of companion to hers, but a lot more powerful.

Dad called it the ultimate bike. He had taught her to ride on his, but he didn't want the first bike she owned to be that big. The fact that she could handle his bike, though, gave him added confidence in her safety on the new bike.

This didn't help Mother's feelings.

"I don't care, Justin," she had said. "Gale shouldn't have her own motorcycle. Get her a car."

"She'd rather have the bike."

"It's dangerous and I don't like it."

"She knows all the safety rules, and she takes to it better than butter takes to corn bread."

"Why can't she be more like Donna."

The magic words. He grinned quickly, then grew serious. "Listen, Della, Gale and Donna are two different people. I love them both the way they are, but Gale is not going to imitate Donna."

"Thanks to you," she said.

"What do you mean by that?"

She hesitated. "You know what I mean."

"No, tell me."

"You've tried to make her like you because we never had a son."

A long moment passed, and in the next room Gale held her breath.

"I'm going to forget you said that." He spoke softly and evenly.

"You wanted a boy, and you've treated her like a boy ever since she was born."

"You're upset; you don't really mean that. I would never change anything about Gale. I'm glad she's a girl. I would rather have her as my daughter than have ten sons. But I've given Gale the opportunity to like things that I like, and do things that I do. I did the same for Donna. But Donna wasn't interested in what you'd call 'boy things.' Gale was. I have never forced either one to be other than what they naturally wanted to be. Gale is like she is because she's Gale. Period."

"But look at her. She hunts and rides motorcycles. And look at the way she dresses, showing no interest in parties or meeting new friends or dating. I mean, by the time she was sixteen I had hoped she'd change."

"To be more like Donna? And you?"

She stared at him.

"Don't you think Donna is more normal?" she asked.

He shook his head. "No," he said. "Sometimes I think your image of the world is the way it was fifty years ago. Gale has more freedom today to develop naturally. Let Gale be Gale, and Donna be Donna. And don't worry that one is different from the other, or different from you."

"I guess nothing I say will change your mind about the motorcycle."

"She has her heart set. I won't disappoint her."

Gale had quietly moved back to her room, closing the door behind her and falling on the bed. She loved her mother, but she had always felt closer to her dad. From the time of her earliest memories she had always felt a closeness to him that she sensed existed between her mother and Donna. She had always been physically active. Growing up she had liked playing basketball with the boys—climbing trees, jumping off roofs, riding horses, hiking and camping, and exploring haunted houses when boys were fearful. She had even had her share of fights in supporting a viewpoint. But she had never thought of herself as "different."

She was different from Mother and Donna, but they were the ones who were "different."

Except, lately, she *had* been feeling different. About boys. They had begun to look more interesting to her, especially—one boy. In the past she had watched other girls act crazy around boys, and say silly things to each other about their dates. But she had her own friends who were boys, and they treated her just like she was a normal person. In fact, she felt a degree of contempt for girls whose world seemed to revolve around what boys said or did.

Her best friend was Danny Moeller. They were in the same class and both wanted to be journalists. Actually, Danny wanted to be a novelist someday, while Gale wanted to become a syndicated columnist writing on national and world issues. But they both figured they'd spend time first as staff reporters on a big-city newspaper. They both were on the staff of their high school paper.

They had gone on "dates" to movies, and the fact that some girls whispered about Gale and her nerdy friend didn't bother her. She didn't care what they thought or said, because Danny was a good friend. They could tell each other things and never worry about anyone else's knowing what they said. They were always there for each other. But lately—and this was troubling to Gale—Danny had begun acting funny with her. He had tried to hold her hand at the last movie they went to, making her feel uncomfortable. And then he tried to kiss her good night. She had pulled away and embarrassed him and the night ended badly with her thinking "no more dates with Danny."

But the weird part was—she kind of knew how he felt. Because she had been thinking about Arnie Stover, and she knew if she tried to kiss him, he would rebuff her in the same way she had Danny.

Arnie was her sister Donna's boyfriend. Gale had seen him a lot when he came to the house to pick up Donna. It was natural to see them together. Donna had always been attractive to boys, with a figure and face made for modeling school. In fact, she was thinking of modeling as a career, making plans to attend a school in New York after graduating next spring. Arnie, certain to get a football scholarship at a Big Ten school, was one of the outstanding high school tight end prospects in the country.

Donna could have had her pick of boys, and chose Arnie. Gale could see why. She had always been aware of his broad shoulders and chest, trim waist, chiseled face topped by blond wavy hair, but lately she had noticed the way one corner of his mouth curled up more when he smiled, the way his blue eyes seemed to get darker when he talked about football, and the way his laughter sounded a little like music. And Gale was aware of how her stomach felt when he came in the house and said something to her.

Last year as a sophomore Gale had looked at him and seen just a good-looking guy with muscles. Now, going into her junior year, Gale saw something more and didn't understand it or like it.

Donna's boyfriend, for goodness sake! Gale wasn't a bit like her sister and was proud of it. Why would she like the same boy as her sister? She got angry thinking about it. But what she didn't understand was the full nature of her anger. What she didn't admit outwardly was the thought that she was no competition for her sister when it came to catching the interest of a boy. Her sister would always win. And Gale didn't like to lose to anyone, especially to her sister.

Now Gale put on her black helmet. Her schoolbooks were in the saddlebags. School! Having to start school two weeks before Labor Day—the pits. Too many bad weather days off last year had forced the early opening. But school shouldn't start until after Labor Day. It was summer. Swimming pools were still open. That's where she'd like to be—swimming. At least she could look forward to the Labor Day bash at the lake. She'd swim then.

She pressed the button and the motor revved quickly to life. Her right hand twisted on the handle and she felt the throb of power echo to her demand. She thought of her sister, who had just left for school in Arnie's car. Donna would never appreciate the thrill of freedom that comes from riding a bike. Then she thought of Danny. She was supposed to pick him up. The last movie date made her reluctant to get him. But he was the first passenger she had carried on her new bike, and she had promised to pick him up for school while the weather was good. She just hoped he wouldn't look at her goofy.

Now if *Arnie* looked at her that way—

But forget it. Sex made everything complicated. Actually, though, she was a little flattered that Danny found her attractive—that way. If Danny did, maybe other boys could?—would?

Maybe Arnie?

No. Move it. School awaits. She gunned the motor

and the rear wheel squealed and inside the house her mother, watching from the window, grimaced and looked at her husband with an "I told you so."

"Don't worry about her," he said, "she's a good driver."

"I wouldn't have to worry if you had got her a car."

"Her time's coming for that. She wanted the bike first."

She poured him some coffee. "You give her too much."

"No more than Donna. One of the reasons I've worked so hard is to be able to give things to our children."

He sipped the coffee. "When Donna gets to New York, that's when you can worry."

"Donna's very sensible. The modeling school is perfectly reputable, and if things don't work out, she's prepared to study landscaping at Georgia Tech."

"I know. But New York's a big place."

Della smiled. "Donna deserves a chance at modeling. Very few girls are blessed with her looks. And if she were successful, she not only would make a lot of money, but she'd have the opportunity to travel and see much of the world. It's a long shot, but why not take it?"

"She's beautiful enough, all right."

"She wants to get into landscaping anyway. Modeling would just delay it a few years." She swallowed some coffee and put the cup down. "You know, you're the reason she wants to go into landscaping."

"She's grown up with it," he said.

"But you made her like it. The way you let her help you when she was growing up, the way you talked to her, encouraged her—made her feel like she had some talent."

"She does. She's got a real flare for it."

"The thing is," Della went on, "I think she's always been jealous of Gale."

"You're kidding."

"Think about it. Gale was the tomboy. She was the one who came closest to being your son. She got most of your attention away from work. She's the one you taught to hunt, the one who jumped into the pickup truck with you."

"I just tried to accept each girl the way she is. Gale was roughhouse; Donna was lunch at the Garden Club."

"I think Donna wanted to be more like a picnic lunch."

He shook his head. "Don't leave yourself out of it."

"What do you mean?"

"I mean *your* influence on Donna. She has always wanted to be like you. And jealousy may cut both ways. Gale is bound to be a little jealous of Donna, especially now that she's getting older."

"You mean about the way Donna looks?"

"About Donna's looks *and* the way she attracts boys."

Gale beeped in front of Danny's house, a colonial white two-story with green trim. Danny came running out of the house, and Gale took his two books and put them into a saddlebag. Then she handed him the extra helmet that was clipped behind the seat. He put it on and straddled the seat behind her.

"Hold on," she said. His arms came around her

waist. She revved the motor and he jerked backward as they took off.

"Let's let it out," Danny said. Gale grinned. Danny looked like a nerd, but he didn't act like one. They got to an open stretch of road and she cranked up the revolutions for a sudden burst of acceleration. Danny held on and laughed. Gale reflected that Danny was game for about any adventure except diving off the twenty-foot platform at the lake. He could not swim well, and diving was something he had always shied away from.

When they pulled up in front of the school Danny's voice was admiring. "That bike is great."

She clipped the helmets to the bike and added locks to them, then took their books from the saddle-bags.

"See you in the cafeteria?" he asked. She hesitated. He rushed his words, "I forgot. I've got to meet with Sam Kennedy and help him with some trig. First week of school and he's already struggling."

"Sure." Gale smiled at him. "I'll see you at the staff meeting."

"Yeah." He turned way and glanced back. "Bye."

"Bye," echoed Gale, feeling relief. She still liked Danny, but not—that way. She wanted things to get back to normal, and knew they would in time.

As Gale opened her locker Renee Watkins came up. Renee was her best friend after Danny. "Did you hear? Crystal Talbert almost drowned last week."

Gale hadn't heard.

"At the lake. She tried to swim all the way across."

"Didn't someone go with her?"

"She just took off on her own. You know how good a swimmer she is."

"What happened?"

They were walking toward British Lit, a class they shared before homeroom. "She had been talking to her boyfriend and he said she couldn't make it across. She said she could. They argued. She just took off."

"What did he do?"

"He watched her go. And according to what I heard, he kept thinking she'd swim back. But she didn't, and then he got a rowboat and began to follow her. Finally, he could see that she was having trouble, but he was so far away he couldn't reach her until she went down."

"You're kidding!" Gale exclaimed.

"He had to dive for her and then in the boat he had to give her mouth-to-mouth resuscitation."

"She's all right?"

"Yes."

Gale grinned. "I bet he didn't mind the mouth-to-mouth part."

Renee laughed. "That lake is too wide to swim across."

"Pete Rankin has done it."

"Look how strong he is. Crystal is—" her voice faded out.

"Crystal is a girl?" Gale asked. "Is that what you were going to say?"

"Crystal's not as strong."

"When it comes to endurance a woman is just as strong as any man. I could swim it."

"If you try, just be sure someone goes with you."

At lunchtime Gale and Renee went through the cafeteria line. Gale saw her sister eating with Arnie.

"They make a good-looking couple," Renee said.

"Let's go sit by them," Gale said, moving with her tray.

"They don't look like they want company." But she followed after Gale.

"Mind if we sit?" Gale asked, then sat before Donna could reply. Donna looked less than enthusiastic, but Arnie was friendly.

"Hello, kid sister," he said. "Renee, have a chair." He pushed back a chair and Renee hastily sat. Then he looked at Gale.

"I like your bike."

"Would you like to ride it?"

"Sure."

Gale looked slyly at Donna. "You could take Donna for a ride."

Donna's brow was a storm cloud. Arnie laughed.

"You mean she hasn't ridden it yet?" He looked at Donna, who took a bite of green beans.

"I think she's waiting for someone she wants to put her arms around," Gale said.

Arnie laughed again. "That's what a bike is good for. Want to go for a ride with me, Donna?"

"I hate motorcycles," Donna said, "and you know I hate motorcycles."

"I think she's afraid her hair will get blown," Gale said.

Donna stared at Gale. "Some of us have better things to do than ride motorcycles."

"Hon—lighten up," Arnie said. "We were just teasing."

"If you want to ride a motorcycle, maybe you'd better date my sister."

"Hey—I'm not riding a motorcycle. The coach

would have a fit. No one on the team can ride a motorcycle until the season is over."

"Of course," Donna said, "the coach won't let you ride. What I want is beside the point."

"No, I didn't mean that," he said.

"You'll never get me on a motorcycle."

"I won't try."

Donna took a last swallow of her iced tea. "I have to get to class early." She stood up, and Arnie quickly rose.

"Will I see you tonight?" he asked.

"I have to study," she said.

"Let me come over. I could use some help on advanced algebra."

"Talk to her," she said. "Gale's the whiz on math, and motorcycles." She walked away, and Arnie sat down slowly.

"What happened?" he asked.

"Welcome to the family," Gale said. "We get into that kind of discussion all the time at home."

"But why is she so touchy about motorcycles?"

Gale smiled. "Because I've got one."

When classes ended the paper staff met for their weekly planning meeting. Mr. Herbert Bennett, journalism teacher and their faculty sponsor, was speaking.

" . . . now, is everyone clear on his assignment?"

Gale held up her hand. "Are you sure you want me to interview the president of New Life?"

"Why not you?" he asked.

"It's just that I haven't been interested in their activities."

"They're one of the most active groups on campus."

"I know, but they're a little too religious for me.

Betty—" she nodded toward Betty Miller, "—could be more sympathetic."

"We're not turning out a PR puff piece. We're after news, which means objective reporting. You should write it because you're not involved."

"But a prayer vigil—" she let her voice trail off.

"That's what makes it news. They're conducting a prayer vigil for a classmate who is dying in the hospital. You may not believe that prayer helps, but the fact that a group of our students are praying around the clock is news."

Danny held up his hand. "I'll take the assignment, Mr. Bennett."

"You're our sports guy, Danny, and you've got a heavy interview with the coach."

"I'll do it," Gale said.

Mr. Bennett smiled. "Good."

That night after dinner Gale called Tina Willard, the president of New Life. They arranged to meet at 8:00 P.M. at the Second Avenue Methodist Church, where the prayer vigil was being conducted.

"Come to the parking lot in back," Tina said. "I'll be at the door looking for you and let you in."

Gale was buttoning her lightweight jacket when her mother said, "Be careful, Honey."

"You sure you have to go out tonight?" her father asked.

"This is the best time," she said, and blew a kiss his way. As she was leaving she heard her sister's voice calling to her mother, "Are you sure Arnie didn't call while I was in the shower?"

Gale grinned to herself as she shut the door behind her.

The Second Avenue Methodist Church had celebrated its one hundredth anniversary only two months before. Six steps led up to a concrete portico which supported four huge round columns that in turn supported an inverted V roofline with a lighted cross in the middle. Gale rode around to the back parking lot. She stopped the bike near the door and saw Tina standing just inside.

Gale wasn't any happier about the interview than she had been in the afternoon meeting. For one thing, she knew Candice Sutton, the girl who was dying of leukemia in St. Mary's Hospital. Gale didn't like dwelling on her condition. But her main reluctance was due to the group itself.

New Life was an interdenominational religious club on campus made up of conservative students. The law wouldn't let them congregate on school grounds for a religious observance, so they were conducting the prayer vigil in the church. Gale could appreciate their concern for Candice and their desire to do something concrete. For them, "prayer changes things." But Gale didn't believe that and was always uncomfortable in the presence of anyone who did.

Tina opened the door for Gale and led her to a deserted room next to the chapel. When they were seated Tina said, "I wasn't too clear on what you wanted to talk about."

"We want to run an article on New Life—its purposes and activities. But what you're doing right now—the prayer vigil—has human interest appeal, and we'll lead with that and spread out to the general material."

Tina nodded, and Gale began to ask questions: When did the prayer vigil begin? Whose idea was it? How many persons were cooperating in the vigil?

Was more than one person in the chapel at the same time? Did Candice know about the prayer vigil? What did her parents think of the idea? Then Tina said something that made Gale stop writing.

"I know that Candice will die," she said. Gale wondered, if Tina felt that way, then why conduct a prayer vigil?

"An angel asked us to," she said.

"You saw an angel?"

"In a dream. He asked us to pray for Candice."

"But if she's going to die—"

"The angel said that prayers would bring comfort. So New Life is praying twenty-four hours a day."

"Have other members of New Life seen an angel?"

"I don't know. But they believe that I have."

"What does an angel look like?"

"In my dream the angel could have been either a man or a woman. He had on a long robe; his hair was long; his face was unshaven. But I believe an angel can appear in any guise."

"Do you believe that you have a guardian angel?" Gale asked.

"Yes," Tina said, "and I believe that you have one, too."

That night when Gale got home her parents were already in bed, and when she went to her room she noticed a light on under Donna's door. She tapped twice.

"Come in." Donna's voice sounded muffled.

When Gale entered she saw an apparition combining hair curlers, mud-packed skin treatment, fresh fingernail polish, flowered gown, and pink bedroom slippers.

"Whatcha wan?" The mud pack had hardened, and Donna couldn't move her face to talk.

Gale sat on the bed. "Did Arnie ever come by tonight?"

"No."

"How well do you like him?"

"Goin steaduh."

"You were hard on him today."

"Your faul."

"No. You acted like you were looking for something to get on him about."

Donna held up her hand, and then stood and went to the bathroom. She came back with clean cheeks that were slightly flushed from the treatment. "Why are you asking these questions about Arnie?"

"Just curious."

"Do you like Arnie?"

"Of course not. Not that way."

Donna laughed. "I've seen you looking at him. You like him!"

"No."

"Would you like me to cast him aside so you could get him?"

"Don't be silly."

"I think being silly would be to believe you'd have a chance with Arnie."

"I'm not interested in Arnie."

"You'd have to catch his interest with more than a motorcycle."

"You're prettier than I am, but there's more to people than the way they look."

"In your case, I hope there's a lot more," Donna said. Gale turned and walked out the door.

During the next few days Gale worked hard on the

article. She didn't want it to sound like New Life was a group of kooks. But she did mention Tina's dream about an angel who had requested prayer for Candice, and the fact that Tina believed she had her own personal guardian angel. Her manner of writing all this, without any tone of skepticism creeping in, was a challenge that taxed her skill to write objectively. She did not, of course, indicate Tina's feeling that Candice would die. She did want to generate good feelings about an organization which cared enough about a dying student that it would mount a continuous prayer vigil.

Right after she turned in the article word came that Candice had died. Mr. Bennett handed the article back to her, complimenting her and then asking her to add the facts and circumstances of Candice's death.

As Gale revised the article she thought again of the angel in Tina's dream. Had the prayers really helped Candice? Did the angel appear to Candice as well? To get those facts she'd have to interview Candice herself. Something, Gale thought wryly, that would be difficult. Some things a reporter is not equipped to find out. Not even the best reporter, she thought, which she intended to become.

Before long she felt more comfortable with Danny. He seemed to accept the fact of their platonic relationship. They had a lot of common interests, and the old rapport that allowed both of them to be open in what they said and thought was too precious to be tossed away by misguided hormones.

Her relationship to Donna didn't smooth out so easily. Both kept their guard up, like two boxers warily circling each other. They had to live in the same ring, but neither wanted to be the first to call time, turn her back, and go to her corner for rest. Donna did a little better with Arnie though. Soon he was coming back to the house for study sessions.

The thing was, Gale felt ill at ease in his presence. Her imagination made her wonder if she saw a new and meaningful glint in Arnie's eyes when he looked at her. She was only a year younger than Donna—not the proverbial kid sister. And she was more intelligent than Donna. Surely he could see that.

But he never outwardly let on that he was having new thoughts about which sister was the more desirable. And she didn't worry about it. That was *his* problem, she told herself. She found herself musing about her clothes. Normally she wore jeans. They suited her inclination and certainly were comfortable on her bike. But—she had good legs. She had nothing to hide there—

She tested different skirts before the mirror. A skirt and matching sweater ... maybe that single gold strand around her neck that Mother had given her for Christmas. How would that outfit look on her bike? Maybe Danny could give her a ride to school for a change, in his '87 Celica ...

Labor Day weekend was approaching fast.

"I really like that outfit." Danny looked admiringly at Gale as they were walking to his car after school.

"You told me that this morning."

"Yeah. Well—" his voice faded.

"You like my legs?" she asked.

"Sure!"

"So are you going to stare at me at the lake?"

He was flustered. "No—"

"I'll go with you but you've got to promise not to start acting funny again."

"O.K." he said. "You make it difficult. I mean—I think you look great. I can't go around with my eyes closed whenever I'm with you."

She smiled. "I've got a new swimsuit, and I don't want your eyes bugging out."

He said nothing else, but as they reached his car he noticed his heart was beating faster.

On Labor Day Gale's parents left for the lake ahead of her. Justin wanted to get to their picnic location early, to make certain that all employees of Hunter's Nursery and Landscaping, Inc., along with their families, would be adequately served during the annual barbecue and beer bonanza. Gale wore her new swimsuit under jeans and T-shirt. Leaving her room, she passed Donna emerging from the bathroom.

"See you at the lake," Gale said.

"Arnie and I may decide not to go."

Gale frowned. "You've got to make an appearance, at least. Dad expects his family to be there."

"I hate his annual picnics."

"If Mom can stand it, you can."

The sky was cloudless, and while positioning herself on the seat, Gale thought this was the perfect day for bike and bash. The bike started immediately with the touch of the button, and responded with a happy growl to a quick twist of the wrist. Foot pressure into first gear and the left hand letting out the clutch—the bike took off like a rabbit-chasing greyhound.

She picked up Danny, and with his arms tight around her she let the bike unwind close to redline when she got on the freeway.

The shoreline of the lake was crowded with cars and people. Hunter's Nursery and Landscaping had reserved picnic area number 23, and was easy to spot thanks to a banner that was strung between two trees. Tables were pushed together to make one long eating space, while various cookout grills were busily emitting smoke from the frenzied efforts of men and women singeing hot dogs and burgers. A small booth was the source of beer and soft drinks on demand. Small kids were being chased by harried mothers to complete the picture of Labor Day fun.

Gale pulled up by a grill where her father was working.

"Where's Mom?" she asked. He motioned toward the tables where women were stacking paper plates and cups and plastic utensils.

"Can I help?" Gale asked.

Justin grinned. "We've got it under control. Just have fun."

Gale moved down to the water with Danny. She could see the far shore across the lake, people looking like moving pinpoints as they mirrored the activity on this side. She could swim it. She would, one day.

A section of the shore had been roped off for swimming. The rope extended with buoys into the water, stretching out to a wooden platform that marked the limit of the swimming area.

"Let's go in," Danny said.

"Later," Gale said. They sat on a log and watched the swimmers. Finally Gale stood and began to take off her T-shirt. Then she began to lower her jeans. Danny stared. He couldn't help it. Gale was wearing

a two-piece red bikini. He knew his mouth was hanging open as Gale straightened up.

"Let's get some sun," she said, and moved toward
the water. Danny rose and walked behind her like a
robot on remote control. Gale stopped thirty feet
from the water and lay on the sand. Danny quickly
sank beside her.

"Nice suit," he said. She didn't reply. "Your folks
seen it?" he asked. She still said nothing. He sighed
and closed his eyes, trying to meditate on the soft
breeze that brought solace to his skin, warmed by the
sun's unblinking gaze. Sometime later he was aware
when she sat up. He propped himself on one elbow
and saw someone approaching.

"You made it," Gale said as Donna and Arnie
stopped beside them. Danny didn't like the way
Arnie was staring at Gale.

"Where did you get that suit?" Donna asked.

"Don't you like it?" Gale asked.

"I do," Arnie said. Donna's lips grew thin.

"I don't think I'd go to the picnic wearing that."

"I'll cover up," Gale said, "but this suit is for
swimming—something you don't seem prepared for."

Donna was wearing a bodysuit under a short skirt
and loose shirt knotted at the waist.

"I could swim in this bodysuit, but Arnie and I are
going to row across the lake. Some friends of his are
on the other side."

"You see the folks?"

"That's why we came to this side first."

"Clever idea," Gale said drily. "Why don't you
swim across the lake?"

"Don't be silly," Donna said.

Gale looked at Arnie. He really looked great! "You could swim across, couldn't you, Arnie?"

He looked at the distant shore, his voice sounding doubtful. "I think so."

"I know you're a good swimmer," Gale said, "and I know Donna is a good swimmer." She looked at Donna. "Remember how you used to beat me when we were learning to swim? One lap of the pool and you'd beat me. Then two laps, and you still beat me. Then four laps—remember when you only beat me by just about three feet? That last time. We never raced anymore after that."

Donna turned to Arnie, "Can we go now? We've seen my folks and now we've seen Gale like you wanted. So can we go?"

"OK," he said, then looked at Gale. "I really do like your swimsuit."

"Why do we have to row across the lake?" Donna asked before Gale could reply. "Why don't we just drive to the other side?"

Arnie grinned. "I need the exercise. Rowing is great for the shoulders and back."

"So is swimming," Gale said.

"Yeah," he said, "but I don't know if I could make it across. That's a long way. You really think you could swim it?"

"Yes."

He smiled. "Then I'd say that would make you Superwoman."

"Let's go!" Donna said, walking away. Arnie shrugged, following her."

"He's a jerk," Danny muttered.

"I don't think so," Gale said, staring after him. They watched Donna and Arnie go to the boat rental

by the dock. Arnie helped Donna get in as she carefully sat at one end, facing him as he took the oars.

"Come on," Gale said, suddenly running toward
the swimming area. Danny followed. Gale dived in
and then Danny and they were swimming toward the
wooden platform at the far end of the swimming
area. Gale reached it before Danny, and pulled herself
up in one easy motion. Then they were sitting and
watching the boat with Donna and Arnie moving out
past the limits of the buoyed rope. He was stroking
strongly, moving the boat in a surging glide toward
the distant shoreline.

Gale watched after them for a long time. Finally
Danny touched her arm. "I'll race you back." She
brushed him off. The boat was in the middle of the
lake, still moving smoothly forward.

"I'm going to the other side," Gale said.

"Why?"

"To prove something."

"What?—that you're Superwoman?"

Gale smiled. "I just might be."

"You trying to impress Arnie? Is that it? OK.—I'll
get a boat."

"I'm going to swim," she said, standing.

"I understand, but I'll row with you."

Gale shook her head. "I don't want a boat."

"You're crazy! What if you get tired or get
cramps? You need a boat."

"Superwoman doesn't need a boat." She dived into
the water like a flashing red tornado, stroking with
little splash and leaving a wake from a gentle butter-
fly kick.

"Come back!" Danny called. Several nearby swimmers looked at him curiously. Danny dived and

started swimming back to the shore. He splashed out
and ran to the boat ramp. The attendant told him all
the boats were out, but one was expected back in ten
minutes. Danny paced the dock, looking toward the
lake, where a moving shape was rippling the water
moving farther and farther from the shore. Five minutes. No boat. Ten minutes. The figure in the water
was still moving, smaller and smaller. Twelve minutes. Still no boat.

"Why isn't the boat here?"

The attendant shrugged. "They don't always keep
track of time." Fifteen minutes. Then Danny saw the
boat, a teenage boy and girl laughing as they maneu-
vered the boat to the dock. Then Danny was in the
boat, grabbing the oars as the boat tilted side to
side. The attendant gave him a shove, and Danny was
rowing.

He wasn't even sure if he would have the strength
to row all the way across. Speeding as fast as he
could would tire him faster and he might never get to
her. But if he slowed, she might go down before he
could reach her. She was crazy! All because of wanting to impress Arnie. She had never been interested
in boys before, and he had never been interested in
girls. Now he was interested in her, and she was interested in someone else.

But none of that mattered now. A gut instinct told
him that she was heading for trouble, and above all
else, he didn't want her in this kind of trouble.

Gale was still stroking smoothly, but she had
slowed down considerably. She was almost halfway
across, which she estimated by the size of the trees
on either shore. Halfway meant the point of no return. No reason to think of going back now. Just as

close to keep going forward. But she was a little sorry she couldn't consider returning. Because she was tired. The distant shore looked dismayingly far. In fact, it almost seemed that she wasn't progressing. She was not gaining on the shore. She was stroking and going nowhere. Mistake. She shouldn't have tried it. She should have let Danny row along with her. No life jacket. If she rested by swimming slower, it would only take her longer to get across, and the longer in the water, the more tired she'd get. If she treaded water, she was not going forward, using energy and making no progress. The best thing was to keep stroking, keep stroking to move closer to the shore.

Past halfway, but the shore was still far off. And she was growing more tired by the moment. The thing was—her arms were getting heavy. Stroke, stroke, head to side and into water. Pump, pump. What is fatigue? Something mental. It's all in the mind. Just keep stroking.

What time was it? The arms were getting really heavy. How much longer could she keep swimming? Hey—she couldn't sink. You could float for hours with the old bobbing technique. You could have your hands tied behind your back and your ankles tied and you could not drown, just by keeping your head and bobbing and breathing easily without panic. The body was naturally buoyant. It could not sink. It would naturally float to the surface of the water. No need to worry. You can't sink. That's it.

Keep stroking. She was weary and tired and fatigued, and the shore was still far off. Why didn't things look closer? She could hardly lift her arms. Why was she doing this? She wasn't Superwoman.

She didn't want to be Superwoman. She didn't want to impress Arnie. Why was she concerned about Arnie? Danny was far superior to Arnie. Danny had warned her not to swim across. Why hadn't she listened to Danny? If Danny were rowing beside her, she could hold onto the boat. She could ride in the boat. But Danny wasn't here. Only her arms were moving, but it was so hard to lift them. She had to rest.

Suddenly she was coughing and rearing her head above water, fighting for air. She had swallowed water! She mustn't sink. She had to keep stroking. She couldn't drown. Mother, she'd miss her mother. And Donna, she loved her sister. Donna could have Arnie. She'd miss Donna. She'd miss her father most of all. Poor Daddy. No one to go hunting with him. *I don't want to drown!*

She was too tired to keep going. She knew it. The arms wouldn't go anymore. The legs wouldn't move anymore. She was going down. They say three times and then you go down for the third time and that's it. Had she been down twice already? Once, maybe twice. But the third time—this was it . . .

She felt the strong arm around her waist and then she could breathe again. Her head was above water and she was coughing but she could breathe! Who had her? Was it Danny? She turned her head—not Danny. Some man she didn't know, swimming with one arm as he held tightly to her with the other. She was on her back, looking up at the sky, grateful to be alive and in the hands of a strong swimmer who could pull her forward.

"How much farther?" she asked him. He didn't reply, and she kept quiet. He didn't need to talk.

Needed all his energy to swim. Hoped he could make it. But she knew, she *knew* he wouldn't let her drown. She lost all awareness of time, the only awareness being the steady surging between water below and sky above. She heard a faint voice then. Danny? Was that Danny? Where was he? Then she didn't hear him.

Suddenly the man swimming beside her stopped. He stood and helped her feet find solid ground. She looked and saw the shore! She was across! She stumbled toward the beach. The water was at her knees and then she was on dry land. She laughed. Some picnickers were looking at her curiously. Donna and Arnie weren't anywhere around.

She turned toward the water to thank the man who had saved her, and saw no one, except—a boat fifty yards away, being rowed by a boy whose voice she had heard on the water. Danny.

She looked in all directions. She walked up and down the beach. Where was he? Where was the man who had saved her?

"Gale! Are you all right?" Danny shakily got out of the boat, pulling it onto the beach. He turned to her and looked like he was about to fall. "I lost sight of you. I thought you had drowned."

"I'm all right."

"You made it," he said, "but you shouldn't have tried it. I couldn't get a boat in time, but you should have let me row beside you. You should—"

She interrupted him. "I know."

He stopped talking. "What?"

"I said you were right. I should have let you row beside me."

"Well," he said, "yes—well, you made it. You said

you could swim it and you did." He grinned. "Super-woman."

"That's where you're wrong, Danny. I'm no Super-woman. Someone saved me, kept me from drowning. He pulled me ashore."

"I didn't see anyone."

"Someone who could swim without getting tired."

"Where is he?"

"I don't know."

"Where did he come from?"

"Out of nowhere."

Danny looked perplexed. "Who is he?"

Gale gave him the brightest smile he had ever seen. "My guardian angel," she said.

3

Ralph's Angel

*His angel Raphael was sent to cure them both of
their troubles*

—TOBIT 3:16

Ralph put his pile of books on top of the wall. Then
he gave a little jump, hoisting himself up. His right
arm didn't feel too bad. A little sore, but he thought
the pain was better. Two guys were already sitting on
the wall at the other end. One recognized him and
nodded, and Ralph waved back. Ralph didn't know
him, but he was used to strangers speaking on campus. Maybe more would be speaking if he had played
football or basketball. But Sanders University was
competitive in all its endeavors, and even tennis players got noticed. Particularly when the team was unde-
feated and leading its conference.

Ralph rubbed his right arm slightly below his
shoulder. He had noticed the first discomfort when he
served in practice a month ago. At first he paid little
attention. He lifted weights as part of his training,
and had developed sore muscles before. Now he was

54

practicing hard to improve what one of the local sportswriters called "undoubtedly one of the most powerful serves in collegiate tennis."

But Ralph wasn't thinking about tennis at this moment. He was anticipating that moment when he would see a tall, dark-skinned, chestnut-haired girl who sometimes walked by here on her break between classes. "Rachel Annison," his friend Harry Spenser had pointed out when he made inquiry two weeks earlier in the student center. "She's a transfer from Vanderbilt."

"Do you know her?" Ralph had asked.

"No, but Marilyn knows a friend of hers." Marilyn was Harry's girlfriend. "I wouldn't get too interested," Harry had added.

"Why not?"

"She's dated Jack Billings, and he's put the word out."

"What do you mean?"

"He doesn't want any competition."

Jack was a right guard on the football team. Everyone knew him because he made all-conference and led the league in tackles and quarterback sacks last fall. But he also had a reputation for a volatile temper. And because he had been in a fight his freshman year and almost been expelled when the other student ended up in the hospital, everyone stayed clear of him.

But Ralph wasn't worried about Jack Billings at this moment. He was concerned about his approach—if she came by. He had his American lit book. He could have it open and look up and smile and jump down from the wall and say, "Don't I know you—?"

Sure, and she would look at him like he was an id-iot from outer space. What he didn't want to do was look foolish. So maybe he would just watch her go by this time. Smile and speak, of course, but establish a little basis for familiarity for a later approach.

But he didn't want to wait for a later approach. He had been thinking about her periodically ever since he first saw her. He had found out the name of her dorm, that her major was English, and that she usu-ally was with a couple of friends and came by the student center at this time. "Keep your options open and your powder dry," his father always told him. Good advice. Maybe the only good advice his father had ever given him.

What to do? OK. Open book. Nonchalant. Maybe she wouldn't even come by. She did yesterday. He had seen her from his position at the window inside the student center.

There she was, coming this way. A girl on either side. He wished she had been alone. But hey—you play the cards the way you get them. Except, he sud-denly felt like his hands were sweating and his throat was dry. And his heart—well, it had just learned to play hopscotch.

Sit here and let her go by? Sit here and give her the old boyish smile? Actually speak? He'd have to make a decision soon. She was coming closer, talking energetically to her friends.

She'll never even see me, he thought. *This is stu-pid. I'm getting out of here.* He moved quickly to jump down, but his hip brushed the pile of books and they tumbled off, landing on the ground the same time as his feet. He hurriedly bent down and gathered them and straightened up, and there she was. She was definitely noticing him—and smiling. He smiled back.

"Humpty Dumpty," he said.

She smiled wider as she and her friends moved by. He was left staring after her and feeling as foolish as his worst daydream.

Humpty Dumpty. Brilliant, Ralph, he thought. He looked at the guys on the wall. They were smiling, too. But they weren't as pretty as Rachel.

That night eating dinner he had trouble keeping up with the conversation. The fact was, he was framing another conversation in his mind, one he hoped would go better than the fiasco at the wall.

He was eating at home, his mother inviting him for the standard birthday meal for his brother. The birthday meal was always a special occasion. His mother fixed the favorite foods of the honored son. His father got a meal, too, but Ralph liked Peter's meal better. Peter always wanted meat loaf, with squash, green beans, macaroni, browned whole potatoes, followed by chocolate cake. Ralph's meal was centered around chicken, while his father liked pork chops.

"Is Rayfield going to give you much trouble?" his father asked. Ralph was startled.

"What?"

"Your next match. I've read the Rayfield team is tough."

"Kindricks is the main problem. We'll be ready."

"How's the arm?"

"Better."

His father drank some tea. "If the soreness hangs on much longer, we need to see someone else."

"Dr. Matthews knows what he's doing."

"He's all right for a sports medicine doctor. But the soreness shouldn't hang on so long."

"I told you it's better." Ralph felt the edge in his own voice. Every conversation with his father always ended up that way. Joseph P. Walker, respected criminal trial lawyer, known for his adversarial style in the courtroom, also was known by his family for the same style at home. He always thought his opinions were the best, and he insisted others think so, too. Ralph's unthinking reaction was to argue back. Peter's was to say nothing and conform.

Ralph had heard every argument why he shouldn't go to Sanders University. First, it was a local school. Ralph would benefit by going out-of-state where he would be more on his own. Second, Sanders's law school was not first rate. Joe wanted Ralph someday to join the Walker law firm, which Joe's father had founded. Third, Ralph's academic record would get him accepted practically to any school. And fourth, Joe could afford to send him anywhere. Ralph's reaction was that he had always liked Sanders. Sanders had offered him one of their few tennis scholarships that paid full tuition. He could live on campus and "be on his own." And he wasn't sure about being a lawyer. He was leaning toward law enforcement.

It had been rough. And because they weren't in a courtroom, Joe had eventually lost. He was proud of his son, though, and watched almost all of Ralph's matches. Besides, he had another son who was more reasonable, who would carry on the Walker tradition.

Ralph glanced at his brother. As usual, Peter had said little during the meal. What his father didn't know was that Peter had no intention of becoming a lawyer. He wanted to be an artist. He had always demonstrated graphic skills.

Ralph remembered one time in the third grade bringing home a drawing of a ship. He had been proud, and Mother spoke the normal supportive words of praise. Ralph thumbtacked it on the corkboard in his room. The next day when Ralph came home from school he went to his room and saw another drawing, thumbtacked next to his. It was a ship more perfectly formed, more carefully drawn, with more attention to details of design. Even an eight-year-old could recognize its superiority. But the eight-year-old had trouble understanding how a six-year-old could draw it.

Peter eventually would have to make his own case, but right now Ralph was more concerned about the case he wanted to make with a chestnut-haired girl.

"Ralph," his mother said, "after dinner would you come with me to the meditation room?"

Ralph glanced at his father, who grimaced. "Sure, Mother," he said. This was one subject that his father never talked or argued about. He had done his arguing when the architect was designing the house. Ralph could vividly recall one conversation when he was looking at house plans with his father and mother.

"That's wasted space, Anne," his father said. "You can go to church when you want to meditate or pray."

She was adamant. "I need that room," she said. "We all need that room."

Normally she never would have argued with her husband. But for this one thing she fought.

"You want a room upstairs just for meditating?

You want a built-in padded bench and a cross on the wall at one end?"

"And a small pedestal in front of the cross with a spotlight in the ceiling that always shines on it."

"Why?"

"Jesus had to leave us, but he left his angels."

"I know you believe in angels, but do you think an angel will be on that pedestal?"

"It's a symbol. When we enter the room we'll be reminded that an angel is present."

"But how do you know that?" his father asked.

"I've told you of the dreams I've had."

"But they were *dreams,* Anne."

"Angels come in dreams. They can come in different ways."

His father had quit arguing then. The room was built, and his mother spend thirty minutes after every dinner in that room. And sometimes, like now, she asked someone to go in with her. This only happened when there was something really serious to discuss, or pray about.

"Mother, I need to phone someone. Can we go in after I make the call?"

"Of course."

Ralph glanced at his father again, who was looking down at his plate and finishing up. "Isn't it about time for that chocolate cake?"

Later Ralph was facing the phone in his old bedroom. Maybe he should have gone with Mother first. He sure didn't want to pick up the phone. He had that weird feeling again that victimized him on the wall. Ridiculous. He was standing here safe in his own room. The only thing he need fear was fear itself.

Sure. So pick up the phone.

First the phone book. University . . . Rawlings Dorm. Push the buttons. Count the rings.

"Hello." A woman's voice, laughter in the background.

"I'd like to speak to Rachel Annison, please."

More ringing. A wait. Then a faint "Hello."

"Rachel?"

"Yes." Voice firmer now.

"I—I met you today." Silence. "I mean—you remember, on the wall. The books falling. The guy that picked them up was me."

More silence. "Humpty Dumpty?"

"I remember."

"My name's not really Humpty Dumpty. It's Ralph Walker."

"That's nice."

She wasn't making this any easier. "I'm a sophomore, and I would really like to meet you. Formally. If we could get together. At the student center? I mean, I'm safe, really. My mother loves me."

She laughed. "You're on the tennis team."

"How do you know?"

"I asked. One of the girls I was with knew who you were."

"Great, but could we meet somewhere?"

"The student center sounds like a good idea."

"Tonight?"

"I'm supposed to be studying, but maybe a few minutes."

"Nine o'clock?"

"All right."

After she hung up Ralph stood holding the phone and staring at a photo of himself about to serve in a municipal tennis tournament three years ago. He felt like he had just completed match point at 40–love to win the championship.

He found his mother in the kitchen. "Just a moment," she said, starting the dishwasher. Ralph followed her upstairs to a room at the end of the hall. The lighting inside was indirect, soft and diffuse. One small recessed spot shone down on a pedestal standing below a wall-mounted wooden cross. Ralph sat and his mother sat beside him. She took his hand, and bent her head in silent prayer. After a few moments she looked solemnly at Ralph.

"I had a dream last night."

Ralph waited.

"I saw an angel and he warned me about your arm."

"Mother, it's better."

"He told me you would know pain, but you must have faith."

Ralph worried about his mother sometimes. He didn't like to think of her going into orbit over religion, but—"What else did he say?"

"He told me to have courage." She studied his face. "Ralph, I want you to go to a specialist about your arm."

Great. Doctor, I'm here because my mother dreamed she saw an angel.

Ralph took his mother's other hand. "It's just a sore muscle. It'll be all right."

"Please—"

"Look, if it gets worse, I promise I'll go to someone else."

After a moment she slowly nodded. "You have an angel, too, you know."

"I will go to another doctor if the arm gets worse. I promise."

Ralph's watch said 8:50 as he was walking on campus toward the student center. He was worried about his mother. She always let his father call the shots, make all the decisions. She never stood up for herself, except in this one area. Her faith offered her the one place where she wasn't afraid to stand up in opposition to her husband. The trouble was—she seemed to be getting more involved with strange ideas, like angels. She'd always believed in them, but dreaming about them so much—

He moved up the steps toward the center, smiling to himself. Dreaming about angels? The only angels were on earth, and they had names like Michelle, Irene, Dorothy, and maybe—Rachel.

Inside he walked past Ping-Pong tables toward a lounge area of plush, thick couches, a fireplace, and a large TV screen. He took a seat against the wall near a ficus tree. He idly looked around, watching the flow of students coming and going, talking in small groups, talking politics, sharing gossip, bemoaning certain professors, laughing at a joke, and trying to impress someone special. He rubbed his arm. It was hurting. He hoped it was getting better, but the discomfort seemed to come and go.

He saw her the moment she came through the doorway. She was wearing a two-piece outfit, the top being green-and-white stripes with a button placket, the bottom a solid green skirt. She was wearing green flats, but still managed to be taller than most of the other girls. Perhaps five-foot ten, he thought, as he stood up and moved toward her. She smiled at his admiring glance.

"I'm Rachel Annison," she said, holding out her hand. "And you're Humpty Dumpty?"

"Ralph Walker." He smiled. Her hand felt good. "Would you like a Coke or something?"

"OK."

They made their way to a vending machine. He watched her pop open a can. *Great,* he thought, *now you're drooling over the way she opens a Coke. Planet Earth, come in.* He led her to a couch as far from the TV as possible.

"I appreciate your meeting me like this," he said.

"I needed a break anyway." She looked down at her Coke. "I have to tell you something. I noticed you watching me, I mean before today. I was hoping you'd say something."

"I thought I was being subtle."

"I'm glad you weren't. I just didn't expect anything so dramatic."

He couldn't believe how open she was. He was used to the guarded conversation, the careful maneuvering that took place on first meeting someone.

"I imagine a lot of guys have fallen for you."

"Not off a wall."

He grinned. A girl he could be honest with? A great concept. "I feel a little crazy tonight. Do you mind if we exchange biographies? I'll tell you about my life, family—the important parts. And you tell me about your life. This would save us some time— getting to know each other."

She was silent a moment. "I feel crazy, too. OK. You go first."

Her eyes were brown, and he lost himself in them while he told her about his family, his tennis, his hopes, his uncertainty about his career. Then she talked, and he learned her home was in Bethesda, Maryland; she was an only child, her mother dying when she was nine; her father was a career official in the Commerce Department in Washington D.C.; he had graduated from Vanderbilt University and wanted her to go there; she had attended for one semester to please him, but realized she would rather be at Sanders, which had been her first choice all along.

"The influence of a father," he said.

She nodded. "He's done a lot for me. But I think he was proud when I finally told him how I felt about school. Normally I tell him everything. We're always honest with each other. But I didn't want to hurt him. His blood runs gold for Vanderbilt."

Rachel wanted eventually to teach British literature at the university level. "Not very practical," she said. "But Dad always taught me anything is possible, and that's what I want to do."

He learned other things about her, but the best thing he learned was that she was undoubtedly the most interesting girl he had ever met.

"Your roommate told me you were here."

The voice startled them. They looked up. "Hello, Jack," Rachel said.

"I thought you were going to be studying tonight."

"I did, but I needed to take a break."

Jack turned his head toward Ralph, staring. "Do you now Ralph Walker?" Rachel asked.

"Ralph, meet Jack Billings."

Ralph stood and held out his hand. Jack took it, squeezing hard. Ralph kept his face composed.

"You play tennis?"

"Right."

Jack dropped Ralph's hand, looking Ralph up and

down. They made a physical contrast. Jack was at least six-foot five, weighed around 270, with huge arms, broad shoulders, big chest, and massive thighs. Ralph was a slender six two, weight 190, with arms that gave no promise of being able to power a tennis ball with brutal speed.

Jack looked back at Rachel. "I'm sorry you weren't able to go with me to hear Dead Wall Revery."

"Maybe another time."

"Yeah. Well, I'll be seeing you."

"Good night," Rachel said.

Jack looked at Ralph. "And I'll be seeing you." His eyes lingered a moment before he walked away. Ralph sat back down by Rachel.

"He was one of the first people I met on campus," Rachel said. "Awfully nice, helped me locate some buildings. I dated him once. But I'm afraid he has trouble taking no for an answer."

The next day Harry stopped Ralph in the hall outside Spanish class. "The word's out that Billings is looking for you."

"We met last night, when I was talking to Rachel."

"You're moving on Rachel? I told you how Billings felt about her."

"He's had one date with her, so he owns her?"

"Good logic, but I'd say his size outweighs your logic by eighty pounds."

"I plan to keep seeing Rachel, if she's willing."

"OK. Just be careful."

"Jack won't have to search for me."

"What do you mean?"

"I'll find him before he finds me. We're going to have an understanding."

Harry's expression was a mixture of surprise and a little awe. "Good luck."

That afternoon Ralph walked up the steps to Laffler's Dorm. Coach Laffler was an icon in the history of Sanders football, and while he had been dead for sixteen years, the record of his winning tenure still burned brightly in the hearts of alumni who had donated funds for this special dormitory that housed football players. Ralph got information at the front desk and moved down the hallway to Jack's room. The door was partially open, letting escape the sound of a country tune by Vince Gill. Ralph tapped on the door.

"Enter."

Ralph pushed open the door. Jack was leaning back in his chair, feet propped on desk, and wearing T-shirt, shorts, and socks. He straightened up when he saw Ralph.

"You looking for me?" Ralph asked.

Jack stood up. "How old are you?"

"What does that matter?"

"You want to get older?"

Ralph laughed. "Is that a threat? Are we talking about a fight? I don't think you're stupid. You want another fight on your record?"

"It won't be much of a fight."

Ralph nodded. "You're bigger, stronger. I admit it. But I don't scare. And I'm going to keep on seeing Rachel."

Jack grabbed both of Ralph's upper arms, and raised him off the floor, holding him there.

"What do you think now?"

"Very impressive," Ralph said. "But you're hurting me. Put me down."

"That's the idea," Jack said, but he lowered Ralph. Ralph's right arm was throbbing. At that moment Ralph knew he would go to another doctor. But that was irrelevant right now.

"Mess with me if you want to, but be ready to explain to my tennis coach why I can't play in the next match."

"I won't explain anything, because you're not going to talk."

"I won't have to, because you're not going to touch me."

They both stared at each other. Suddenly Ralph held out his left arm, shoulder width, straight out.

"What are you doing?" Jack asked.

"Do it."

Slowly Jack raised his own arm. "My arm won't go down until after yours," Ralph said.

Jack grinned. "Tough guy, eh?"

They both stood that way. Minutes passed. A guy looked in. "Hey, Jack—" he stopped, staring.

"Close the door," Jack said. The guy looked out in the hall. "Jerry, come here."

Jerry's face appeared. Another face came up behind. Soon there were seven bodies crowding the doorway, watching two men with their arms straight out. Ralph was feeling the strain, and felt a slight trembling. But he smiled at Jack, trying to look as comfortable as a cat curled up on a pillow.

Ralph heard an occasional whisper from the doorway, but he shut all that out now, concentrating only on his left arm. He thought of a tree with a branch, solid and unmoving over the years. The sense of pain was growing more acute. Throbbing, now visibly trembling. But still outstretched. The arm was a block of wood. No strain, pain. Yes, pain, lots of pain. But Jack's arm was trembling, too. Smile. Smile.

How long they stood Ralph had no idea—an eternity? At the very moment when Ralph felt extreme pain, Jack grunted as his arm fell limply. Still smiling, willing his arm not to drop, Ralph used all his control to let his arm down slowly.

The two looked at each other a long moment, and Ralph said, "Thanks, Jack." He walked away through the onlookers, who began asking Jack questions. But what was bothering Ralph was the pain in his right arm, not his left.

That night in bed Ralph dreamed that Jack was squeezing his arms again, but this time Jack's hands were iron claws. Ralph woke from the pain, his right arm still hurting. It eased after about a half hour, and he went back to sleep. But in practice the next day his serve caused a sharp pain that made him lower his racket. He talked to his coach who personally made him an appointment with the sports medicine doctor. A visit there was inconclusive, and Ralph was referred to another doctor. This new doctor took x-rays, tissue samples, and ordered a complete blood analysis. For the next three days Ralph didn't practice, and his mother got him in the meditation room again. They prayed, and his mother turned to him.

"The angel warned us."

"I have the pain, all right."

"He said to have faith. You've got to believe he can help you."

"I hope he can."

"Faith, Ralph, you've got to have faith."

Two days later Ralph was talking to Rachel as they sat beside a large pond sheltered below sloping hills in the city's Hillcrest Park. Actually, the day was a little cool, but Ralph didn't mind the temperature or the recurring gusty breeze that gently whipped Rachel's hair against her forehead.

"They still don't know anything about your arm?" she asked.

"They'll let me know the test results tomorrow."

She took his hand and squeezed it. "I hope everything's all right."

He leaned forward then, gently pressing his lips on hers and it felt like the most natural thing in the world.

The next day his parents were with him in the doctor's office. Ralph was uneasy, for the doctor had requested they all come.

Dr. Malcomb Garroway smiled at his patient, but he hated what he had to say. He knew from experience that the best way was to get it out immediately.

"I'm sorry, but the tests and x-rays confirm that you have a malignancy in your upper right arm. We'll have to operate."

Ralph stared. His mother's lips tightened. His father, typically, was defiant.

"What does that mean?"

"It means without an operation the malignancy will spread. Hopefully we can get it all. We'll follow up with radiation."

Now even his father was silent. The doctor went on.

"I'm afraid the operation will affect the movement of your arm. No more tennis."

Still no one replied.

"We'll get you admitted to the hospital. I've gone ahead and scheduled an operation for tomorrow."

"So soon?" Ralph asked.

The doctor spoke slowly. "I don't want to alarm you unduly. But we need to do this as soon as possible."

For the first time, Ralph knew real fear. His mother squeezed his hand. "Have faith," she whispered.

That night he tried to watch television, but he couldn't get comfortable on his hospital bed. His parents were already gone, assuring him they would see him before the operation. Peter had poked him on his left shoulder, having trouble saying anything. And Rachel had been there. She had sneaked a quick kiss on his forehead. But now he was alone. Except for the tube. He clicked off the TV. Now he was really alone.

He wanted to sleep, but doubted if he'd ever get sleepy. Maybe the best thing was to close his eyes and just drift. Maybe he'd get drowsy and fall asleep. What about counting sheep? What about dogs instead. He liked dogs better. Time passed. Or did it? He didn't know.

He opened his eyes abruptly. Had he been sleeping? How late was it? He didn't have his watch. He looked toward the door and saw a man coming toward him. He was wearing a white scrub suit with a stethoscope around his neck, carrying blood pressure equipment.

"Final checkup," the man said. Ralph didn't recognize him. The man wrapped his arm and took his blood pressure. Then listened to his heart with the stethoscope. "You'll be all right."

"Thanks, doctor."

"You do believe that, don't you?"

"I hope so."

"You do believe that your arm will be all right? That you'll play tennis again?"

"Dr. Garroway said that—"

The man interrupted. "What do you say? Are you going to play tennis again?" He stared into Ralph's eyes, and Ralph felt a warmth that seemed to permeate both arms and legs and then his whole body. Ralph felt like he was floating as he nodded. "Yes. Yes—I'll play."

The man smiled. "Time for you to rest." Ralph suddenly felt fatigued. He closed his eyes, and didn't see the man leave.

Ralph woke with a hand touching his arm. "Blood pressure time," the nurse said.

"The doctor last night said he was making the final check."

"What doctor?" The nurse looked at her chart. "No doctor saw you last night."

"It was late. He checked my heart and blood pressure."

"You were dreaming."

"I saw him."

The nurse shrugged. "Your pressure is fine this morning. The doctor wants some new x-rays, and after that we'll prep you."

"My parents are coming."

"They'll see you. We'll bring you back here before the operation."

After the x-rays Ralph found his parents waiting in his room. The nurse gave him some pills to swallow. "How do you feel?" his father asked.

"Fine. They sure take good care of you here. People check on you at all hours."

"They should, with what they're being paid," his father said.

"The doctor late last night really made me feel better."

"Dr. Garroway came by?"

"No. I didn't know him. The funny thing is the nurse this morning had no record of the doctor's being here."

"What did he look like?" his mother asked.

"Like any doctor. Dressed in white. I sure didn't dream him."

An orderly came in and whispered something to the nurse, and they left the room.

"Son," his father said, "I hope you know we're behind you all the way. I know you'll miss tennis, but—" his voice drifted off.

"You remember what I told you," his mother said. Ralph nodded.

They waited. Finally, his father said, "Peter's in the waiting room. The hospital didn't want anyone but parents up here."

Ralph nodded. More silence. Then the door opened and Dr. Garroway came in carrying x-rays. He looked nervously at the parents and then at Ralph.

"I—I have to say that nothing like this has ever happened in my twenty-three years of practice." He quit talking. No one spoke. He cleared his throat. "We have all the other x-rays, you see. All the other tests. We need to make more tests. More x-rays."

"What do you mean, Doctor?" Ralph's father asked, his naturally belligerent tone creeping in.

Now the doctor looked directly at the father. "I mean, Mr. Walker, that these new x-rays show absolutely no trace of any cancer. If more x-rays and tests confirm it, there is no need for an operation."

Ralph's father looked disbelieving. His mother closed her eyes, and Ralph saw her lips move. As for his own feelings, he didn't need more tests. He knew what they would show. Because he knew the way his arm felt right now. And he knew something else. That man last night had not been a doctor. He could hardly wait to tell Rachel about his guardian angel.

4

David's Angel

The Son of Man will send out his angels
—MATTHEW 13:41

Finishing lunch, his brother announced that he was going to hunt for arrowheads. That's what he said, but David knew better. Douglas was going to head for the creek where the cave was, but after he couldn't see the house he would cut away toward the bluff and head down the mountain to the valley and hike to a clearing in the woods where he would meet Nancy Harrison. But this time David was going to follow him, and he was going to take some pictures. And then he was going to get his brother in real trouble.

Douglas always pretended he didn't like Nancy. David remembered the cracks Douglas made last year about that skinny, pigtailed Harrison girl who lived in the valley. "She thinks she's smarter than anyone else."

But that was last year when Douglas and Nancy were thirteen. Now they were fourteen, and something was happening to Nancy. She wasn't so skinny anymore. And she wore her hair differently, loose and free to move whenever she turned her head quickly. David first had noticed the change one Sunday in church. He had been sitting by Douglas and leaned over and whispered, "Look at Nancy."

Nancy was sitting in the second row of the choir. It wasn't a big choir, only eleven people in it—all ages and sizes, with Nancy being the youngest. But she looked kind of—grown-up. Pretty, even.

Father had nudged him on the head, and he quickly shut his mouth while his brother smirked at him.

The Harrisons were the only family from the valley who attended here. Jeffrey Harrison had lived on the mountain and grown up in this church, and he brought his family every Sunday even though they lived miles away.

Father was what you'd call old-fashioned. He came to church every Sunday and sat in the same place in the same pew and his wife and two sons sat with him. He ruled his family with a strong hand, expecting instant obedience. That's the way he had been brought up on Buck Horse Mountain, living in the same house his grandfather had built and going to the same little Cross River Baptist Church that was stuck in the deep woods at the end of a rutted road.

David never tried to analyze why he and his brother didn't get along. He was too young to think about that. But he did know one thing. Even though they had different interests, they were alike in at least two ways—they both didn't like to lose, and in the face of being wronged, they both wanted to get even.

Probably his Aunt Clara was the one most sensitive to David's own feelings. She had lived with them as long as he could remember. Her family had come to this long, stretched out, miles-long mountain in Georgia in the 1870s. She was one of the two Dickson sisters who survived a locally severe flu epidemic when they were children. The mother died, and two other children. At ages nine and eleven, Ethel and Clara suddenly had been forced to grow up, taking over the cooking and household chores. The country school was three miles away, and they had to walk it every day, cold or hot, rain or shine, until the county finally could afford a school bus by the time they got to high school.

Their father married again when the girls were in high school, but they did not get along with their stepmother. If anything, this conflict tightened the already strong bond between the sisters, strengthening their resolve to start homes of their own as soon as possible.

They ended up marrying brothers who both lived on the mountain. And even more, they married at the same time in the same church, afterward setting up housekeeping on nearby farms.

Then two years later the stepmother died when she stumbled on a slick rock in the creek and hit her head. A year after that their father died of diabetes from complications resulting from having ignored his diet for years. That left the old homeplace vacant, and the sisters decided Ethel and Donald should take it over, since the house was a considerable improvement over the Riggs's place. The sisters divided the acreage between them.

Douglas was born the next year, and that same year Clara's husband died in a hunting accident. Ethel immediately asked Clara to move in with them, and Clara agreed. That was probably the only time when Donald Riggs did not influence a decision made by his wife.

When David was born he came into a home that offered him two mothers. Clara was always close by. She never married again, nor did she ever show an interest in any man. Douglas once said he bet Aunt Clara didn't like her first marriage and that's why she was the way she was. But ten-year-old David secretly thought she loved him too much ever to leave and live somewhere else. There was no question that Clara doted on David, spending hours reading him books and telling him stories from the Bible about battles and miracles and angels.

The angels especially intrigued him. She told him that angels delivered messages from God, and sometimes they helped people. This was why they were called guardian angels. If a person were in trouble or had a special need, then a guardian angel might come and help him.

As a young child David had plied her with many questions about angels. How did they look? Did they fly? Did they really have wings? Were they boys or girls? Are they still alive? Why can't we see them?

On this Saturday everyone sat down for lunch at 12:02. David knew because he checked the time on the new watch his folks had given him for his birthday a week ago. He liked the present Aunt Clara gave him better, though. It was a small autofocus camera. Two feet to infinity, the instructions said. He didn't know what "infinity" meant, so he had asked his aunt.

"As far as you can see," she had said. David always asked a lot of questions. That was one of her

favorite things about him. David didn't get many an-
swers from his father, and his mother seemed to be
busy most of the time. So Aunt Clara took the time
to try and answer everything. His questions a month
before his birthday were what gave her the idea for
the camera.

He had been looking through binoculars that had
belonged to Clara's dead husband. Out behind the
house he focused on the chicken coop, the horse
barn, the cow barn, the farm equipment, delighted
with how things looked up close. But the way he described the things, it seemed to Clara that he had an
unusual eye for a child his age.

"You know," he added, "when you see things close
they look a lot different. You see things you never
saw before."

And Clara clicked on "camera." She had been
wondering what to get him for his birthday. He was
old enough to take photographs, if the camera were
simple enough.

She always had to be careful, though, what she
gave the boys. Her husband's insurance and the sale
of their farm had given her the financial means to
buy more costly presents than the parents could afford. But a camera—that should be all right if it
weren't too expensive.

Clara could visualize the boy becoming absorbed
in finding images he wanted to capture. An explorer
with a camera—with a camera *and* binoculars. Now
that was a combination to expand the imagination of
any growing child, especially one as bright as her favorite nephew!

So she had gone to Dewfield and visited the town's
one camera store. Some cameras were too expensive,

some too complicated. She settled on a compact autofocus with a 35mm f/3.5 lens. "So simple a child could operate it," the clerk said. Clara smiled. "I'll take it."

She knew her sister would still say the camera was too expensive for a ten-year-old boy. But Clara knew that this ten-year-old would take better care of it than most adults would.

During lunch the conversation touched on Father's friend Ned Baxter, who was in the hospital at Marshallton recovering from a stroke.

"I need to drive down and see him this afternoon," David's father said. "But I'm not feeling too good myself."

His mother looked concerned. "Why don't you rest a while, then see how you feel?"

"I might do that."

After the meal his father stood up from the table as did everyone else. David looked at his watch: 12:57.

"All right, Douglas," his father said, "you can go to the creek, but be back in time for milking."

"I will," Douglas said.

"You've been spending a lot of time lately looking for arrowheads."

"It's fun."

David grinned. If Father only knew what kind of fun. Douglas moved toward the front door, and David hurried toward the stairs.

"Where are you going, David?" his father asked.

"To get my camera. I want to take some pictures."

"You be back early, too. And don't wade in the creek when you're carrying that camera."

"Yes, Pa." He ran upstairs, got the camera, took

the steps down two at a time and bounded out the front door.

"Don't slam—" his mother started to say as the door slammed behind him.

He could see Douglas on the path to the creek. He slowed down and let Douglas get farther ahead. He knew where Douglas was going because he had been secretly meeting Nancy every Saturday afternoon for weeks. Now David was going to get proof.

David thought back to that night after dinner when Douglas had invited him into his room, closing the door behind them and putting his finger to his lips. "I want to show you something." Then Douglas got down on his knees and began to feel under his mattress, grinning at David.

"Do you know what a girl looks like?"

"Sure," David said.

Douglas pulled out a magazine. "I bet you don't."

David didn't understand what Douglas meant. Of course he knew what a girl looked like.

"What a girl *really* looks like—" Douglas opened the magazine, "—is this!" He pushed out the magazine so that David was staring at two pages.

"What do you think?" Douglas asked.

David gaped, unable to say anything.

"Take a look at this one." Douglas showed him another page. David turned away and started to leave the room.

"Hey!" Douglas said, "come back here."

David slowly moved to him.

"I'm giving you an early education. Do you want to see more pictures?"

David shook his head.

"Maybe you're afraid to look. Is that it? Are you afraid?"

"No." David spoke softly. "I just don't want to."

"OK. But you keep quiet about this. Don't let on to anyone I've got this. If Dad finds out, I'll know who told him. And no matter how rough he is on me, I guarantee things will go harder on you. Got that?"

David nodded.

Douglas was angry. "I shouldn't have brought you in here. I'd have given anything to see these pictures when I was your age. Go on, get out."

David was confused as he went to his room. Those women looked funny. Interesting looking, but he felt—embarrassed. But why should he be embarrassed? He had sometimes wondered what women looked like under their clothes. In the second grade one time he had been playing on the jungle gym, and Carolyn Michaels had hooked her legs over a bar and hung upside down. She was wearing little white underpants, and he thought about how she might look hanging upside down without clothes on. But the next instant he thought about climbing to the top bar and hanging with one hand.

David knew his father would be upset if he knew Douglas had that magazine. When the preacher talked about sin he'd mention naked women sometimes, and his father would be saying some of the loudest Amens in the church. What was the big deal?

He was curious though. He wondered if Douglas had more magazines like that. He'd better be careful. Father had better not find out.

The real trouble with Douglas started when David entered his room when Douglas wasn't there. He hoped to find the arrowhead Douglas had recently discovered in the cave next to the creek.

Douglas and David had gone inside the cave many times, looking for arrowheads. The story told them by their father was that a tribe of Native Americans had once lived on this part of the mountain, utilizing the cave as a place for making arrowheads. Many arrowheads had been found in the cave. In fact, his father had mounted the arrowheads passed on to him by his father, plus what he, himself, had found, to make an impressive wall display. But the cave and surrounding area had been searched over the years by many other people as well, so that Douglas and David had been unable to find many new ones. The most recent one Douglas found was one of the best.

So on this afternoon, while David was snapping outdoor shots with his camera, he had thought of the arrowhead, and decided he would put it next to an egg and try to get a chicken to be looking at them as they lay side by side in the nest.

David checked the top of Douglas's dresser, then the shelf in the closet. He went back to the dresser and opened the top drawer. He saw a cigar box and opened it. Inside was a pocket knife, a pair of dice, a rabbit's foot, scissors, a Joe Montana football card, and it was there—the arrowhead. David picked it up and closed the drawer. He started to leave and looked at the bed.

He wondered if the magazine were still under the mattress. Perhaps Douglas had a new magazine, or maybe several by now. David was curious. Not that he wanted to look at the women—or maybe he did, a little. It would be easier to look at the magazine if Douglas weren't watching him.

He moved quietly to the door and closed it. Then he moved to the bed and began to feel under the mattress. Nothing. He moved his hand toward the head of the mattress. Then he felt the corner of a magazine. He pushed his hand farther in and pulled it out. The same magazine, but the pages were now more crinkled.

The cover picture began to make him feel funny again. Then he slowly opened the magazine and spent long moments staring before turning to the next page. He sat down. Actually, he thought, these pictures *were* interesting.

He looked up when the door opened. Douglas looked angry as he hurriedly closed the door and rushed to David, grabbing the magazine from his hands.

"What are you doing?"

David quickly stood up. "I wanted to borrow your arrowhead to take a picture."

"Sure, you want to take a picture of my arrowhead," Douglas said sarcastically. "That's why you were looking at this."

David didn't answer.

"You little weasel. What if Father had seen you?"

"I closed the door."

"He could have come busting in. He's in the house now."

"I'm sorry."

Douglas shook his head. "Not good enough. I gave you a chance to look at it, and you were scared. This time of day Father could pop in after getting washed up."

"I said I was sorry."

"I don't like your getting my arrowhead, either. This is my room and you have no business in it."

"You came in my room and got my binoculars the other day."

"Those are Aunt Clara's binoculars."

"She's going to give them to me."

"You think she'll give you everything don't you, Weasel?" Douglas put the magazine back under the mattress. "Mr. Favorite Nephew. Mr. Baby Nephew. Just stay out of my room. Is that clear? And keep your lips zipped about the magazine."

David was angry. "And you stay out of my room!"

"Well—" Douglas said, "—Baby Nephew has a temper. Baby Nephew needs to be taught a lesson." Douglas grabbed David's shoulders and began to shake him. "Don't you ever tell me what to do! Got that, Mr. Baby Nephew?" He shoved David violently away, and David fell into the dresser—sending the lamp crashing to the floor, the glass base splintering on impact.

"Now you've done it," Douglas moaned. He bent down and began picking up the pieces. "Help me," he said, but before David could act they heard their father's voice as the door opened.

"What's going on here?"

Douglas and David stared at him. "David knocked over the lamp," Douglas said. Their father turned to David.

"Is that right?"

"He shoved me," David said.

"I did not!" Douglas said quickly. Their father kept looking at David.

"Did you knock over the lamp?"

"Yes, but—"

"I've told him to stay out of my room," Douglas interjected.

"Were you boys playing roughhouse?"

The boys said nothing.

"Do you remember what I said about not doing that in the house?"

Slowly the boys nodded. "Yes, sir," David said.

"You boys are going to have to pay for the lamp out of your chore money."

"He ought to pay," Douglas said.

"Both of you will pay," Father said. "You can split the cost. Understood?"

The boys nodded.

"All right," Father said. "Clean up the mess." He left the room.

"I should have told him about the magazines," David said in a low voice.

"Do that and you're dead!" Douglas hissed.

"You shouldn't have lied about me."

"It was all your fault."

"But you pushed me, and you lied."

"I'll push you again if you ever come in my room when I'm not here."

That's when the idea began to form in David's mind, a way to get even.

Back in his room David remembered a time several months ago when Douglas had laughed in describing the man-to-man talk his father had given him.

"The old birds and the bees routine," Douglas said.

"What's that?" David asked.

"You're too young to understand, but he'll give you the talk someday. He'll take you aside and tell you what it means to grow up."

"You tell me."

"I'll let him tell you. But by the time he does, you'll know it all anyway." Douglas shook his head. "Father's a real case."

"What do you mean?" The boys were outside, eating grapes at the arbor that was fifty yards from the house.

"You know how he is," Douglas said, "how he feels about women and sex."

"You mean the way he says Amen in church when the preacher talks about sin?"

"Yeah," Douglas said, plopping four grapes into his mouth and then spitting out the seeds. "He's already told me I can't date any girl before I'm sixteen."

"Why do you want to go out with a girl?"

"Because—" Douglas's voice tapered off. "Well, when a girl gets older, and—a boy gets older, they, uh—something changes. They change, or—well, you just feel different about a girl. You'll find out."

"Why does Father not want boys and girls to be together?"

"I guess it was the way he was brought up. He's got crazy ideas. Like no mixed swimming in the river. I'm not going to wait until I'm sixteen."

"What are you going to do?"

"All I'll say is—what he doesn't know won't hurt him." Then Douglas added, "Or hurt me."

But David had followed him one day, all the way to the bluff where the mountain sloped down to the wooded valley below. He stopped, afraid to go farther. But the next time he followed Douglas he didn't stop at the bluff. It seemed to take forever before they reached the valley, and then in the level woods it took forever to break out into a clearing. Then they went into another wooded area. Several times David had ducked behind a tree trunk, thinking that Douglas was going to look back. But Douglas whistled and walked, and David had no trouble staying with him.

He was growing tired when they finally came to another clearing. A huge tree trunk was lying on the ground, and a girl was sitting on it. David was real careful peeking through the leaves, but he recognized Nancy Harrison.

Douglas sat beside her on the trunk. After awhile he held her hand. Then, as David watched, he saw their heads go close together. He continued to watch and all that happened was their looking at each other and talking, and once in awhile their heads seeming to touch. He couldn't hear what they were saying, but faint laughter reached him from time to time.

He got bored.

He would have gone back by himself, but he didn't know these woods and he was afraid he'd get lost. So he waited and waited. Finally the girl moved away from the tree trunk, giving a wave, and Douglas turned and started walking rapidly in his direction.

David had more trouble staying with him on the way back. For one thing it was late and Douglas was moving faster. For another, he didn't whistle as much. By the time they had climbed the mountain and were on a level path to the house, David was exhausted. He decided he wouldn't follow Douglas on any more visits to the valley.

And he hadn't—until now. But he knew Douglas kept going, because several times he had watched him head for the creek and then veer off the path on his way to the bluff. And he could tell by the way

Douglas and Nancy looked at each other in church that they shared a secret.

Out of sight of the house, Douglas left the path as usual, heading toward the bluff. David was glad he was whistling.

David was careful with the camera as it hung around his neck. He'd grab the camera case every time he had to brush by a tree or bush, making sure it didn't swing and bang into anything. He thought about how to get closer to the couple at the tree trunk. He wanted to show their faces. That was going to be a problem. His camera didn't have a zoom lens. But even without close faces, the photographs were going to upset Father. Douglas would learn he couldn't push his brother around!

He followed Douglas to the bluff, then down the mountain. When they reached level ground on the valley floor, the woods thinned out for the next twenty minutes. Then Douglas came to the first clearing, but this time he cut to the right in a different direction from the time David followed him before. He waited just inside the woods while watching his brother cross the clearing. Then Douglas entered more woods, and David moved to follow.

The new woods grew thicker the farther they walked. David couldn't understand where Douglas was going. Then Douglas veered left. In the thicker woods David was having trouble keeping close enough while not making noise that Douglas could hear. The whistling reassured him, but keeping up with Douglas was getting harder. The woods seemed to close in all around him. Nothing was familiar. Everything he saw was new and unknown, and only the

faint whistling and fleeting glimpses of Douglas kept
his mind at ease. But where was Douglas going?

The first moment of worry came when he realized
the whistling had stopped. Douglas had stopped other
times, of course, but he always started whistling
again. And in the sparser foliage David had maintained contact with him. But this time, as he cautiously moved forward and peered ahead, he saw no
sign of Douglas. He kept going, figuring that Douglas
would start whistling again. No sound except an occasional gust of wind topping the trees.

David stopped, listening intently. Nothing. Now he
moved faster in the direction he last saw Douglas.
Then still faster. After a few minutes he stopped and
once more tried to hear any sound of movement or
whistling. Nothing. Now he looked around, wanting
to call out, to yell for Douglas, but his pride firmly
gripped his mouth. Douglas would be mad at him for
following, but that wasn't what David was afraid of.
He was afraid Douglas might laugh at him for getting
lost.

Lost? Was he lost?

He knew what direction he came from, but he had
done a lot of swerving and changing directions, moving through country totally new and unknown to him.
He looked at his watch. He had been walking for
more than two hours. He had no more thought of trying to follow Douglas now. He wanted to go home.

He started out, hoping to see familiar landmarks
that would let him know he was traveling the way he
came. But everything looked different going back.
There was no path to follow, only trees and under-
growth and rotting logs. And nothing looked the
same. But he kept walking, knowing he was not

changing directions frequently as he had done following Douglas, knowing everything looked as though he had never been here before.

He was lost. Admit it. Really lost, and he had no idea how to get back home. Maybe if he kept walking in one direction he would eventually come to a road or a farm. Or maybe he would come upon the upward slope of the mountain. If he climbed up the mountain, he could find a road that would be familiar and he could then get home.

But everything was a guess. No way to know what direction, no way to know directions to anywhere. He couldn't even use the sun to find west, because the sky was overcast. He was lost in the middle of strange woods and he could only keep walking.

After another hour he stopped walking. He was still in the woods, knowing that he had come full circle back to a rock where he had earlier sat and rested. He was tired, and he was getting thirsty. He *was* thirsty! And he wanted to be home. Why had he got that crazy idea to follow Douglas and take pictures of him and Nancy? Sure, he wanted to get Douglas in trouble. He wanted to show Father pictures of Douglas meeting Nancy and putting his arm around her. He wanted to show them kissing. But there were other ways to get even. He'd figure out a better way, a way that didn't drag him out into the woods.

He started running, but after a low-hanging limb scratched his face he stopped. Then he called out for the first time. He yelled for help, again and again. Answering him was only the silence. He started walking again and kept walking and walking and then he was walking and crying. Finally he stopped, exhausted, and sat on the ground with his back against a fallen tree.

What would he do if it got dark? He didn't have any matches, any food. There were still hours of daylight left, but his mind seized upon the thought that he might never find his way out. They would look for him, of course. And his parents would be angry, especially his father. But they might never find him. He might—die here.

He had never been so afraid in his life. He closed his eyes and began to sob. And then his crying stopped, reaching a natural end that left him resting limply against the tree. He didn't know what made him open his eyes.

At first through slits, not seeing clearly, then opening wide. Someone was coming! He could hear the movement of a footfall on fallen dead limbs. Then he saw the shape of a man coming toward him.

Father!

His father had found him! He jumped up and ran, his arms outstretched until they ended up encircling his father's chest.

"How did you find me?" he asked.

"I've been looking a long time."

"But how did you know I was in the woods?"

"I knew." His father ruffled his hair. "Are you all right?"

"Thirsty. But I'm OK now."

His father smiled. "Let's go home."

They began to walk, and David did something he hadn't done in years. He held on to his father's hand.

Somehow the walk back didn't seem tiring at all. Even going up the mountain was easy. And when they came across the main road, they followed it to the familiar fork that led to their house. It was getting dark as they approached the front porch.

"Is Douglas home?" David asked.

"Yes."

David saw his mother appear at the door, and he dropped his father's hand and ran to her. She was distraught, and so was Clara who came up beside her.

"Where have you been?" his mother asked.

"I got lost in the woods, but Father found me."

She looked puzzled as David continued. "I was resting against a tree, and—" David looked behind him, "and Father—" he stopped. "Where is he?"

"Who?" his mother asked.

"Father. He was right there. Where'd he go?"

"Your father isn't here."

"No. Father found me. He brought me home. He was walking with me just a minute ago."

"You were walking by yourself. Your father's been gone all day, remember? He went to visit Ned Baxter in Marshallton."

"No. He was with me. I saw him, talked to him, touched him. It was Father."

Douglas came to the door, grinning at him. "Have a good hike?" he asked. He looked toward the road and they all turned to the sound of a car coming toward them.

"He'll tell you," David said, running to the car as it pulled up. "Tell them you found me," David said as his father got out of the car. "Tell them you brought me home."

"I've been in Marshallton. I told you that at lunch."

David was silent then.

"Is something wrong?" his father asked.

"David just got home," Douglas said. Their father looked at David.

"You know you're supposed to be home way before dark."

"Yes, sir."

"We'll talk later." He moved toward his wife. "Ned's not doing well."

"Dinner's almost ready," she said, moving inside the house with her husband and Clara, leaving the boys on the porch.

Douglas was grinning. "I asked if you had a good hike."

"Not very."

"I did." Douglas chuckled. "I saw you following me. Thought I'd see how far you'd go."

"You led me into the woods so I'd get lost?"

"I didn't mean for you to get lost. I've got to tell you something, though." He took a deep breath. "I was getting worried." Douglas entered the house and David followed him. Clara was waiting inside.

"Please don't worry us like that again," she said. She brushed his cheek with her hand. "Dear boy—I'm glad you found your way out."

"I didn't, Aunt Clara."

"Of course you did."

"No," he said. "You remember what you told me about angels, how sometimes a guardian angel will help you?"

She nodded.

"A guardian angel helped me, and the funny thing is, he looked like my father."

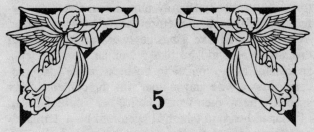

5

Annabel's Angel

Do you suppose that I cannot appeal to my Father, who would at once send to my aid more than twelve legions of angels?
—MATTHEW 26:53

She checked her image in the mirror over the dresser after applying her lipstick. She admitted she didn't understand all the nuances that made up the male concept of what denoted sexy female beauty, but she knew that men thought she was blessed with its natural endowment. All eyes could see the way she looked, and there wasn't much she could do to alter her impact except try to tone it down when she needed to, like today.

She was speaking to a luncheon of Business and Professional Women on the subject of "How a Woman Can Have It All." And she wanted to look like she meant business, not monkey business.

She quickly put on a pale pink blouse, followed by a light gray suit with a medium full skirt that stopped at the knees. A pearl necklace, pearl earrings, skin-toned hose, matching gray pumps completed the effect. Now she stood before the full-length mirror. Yes, she looked like a businesswoman. But Annabel Overstreet also looked like a woman, period. Being successful as a woman in business while also succeeding as a wife and mother was the content of her speech. The women would notice her ash blond hair, of course, her skin (she had been told by a dermatologist that it was flawless), and her figure (jogging two days a week, aerobics three days). But they would also know that she owned and operated a highly popular women's apparel store, and that she was married to a bank vice president and was the mother of a three-year-old daughter.

A child's voice sounded through the hallway door: "Mommy—" Then the child appeared, ponytailed hair the color of her mother's, running and jumping on the bed.

"Down from there." Annabel reached out and the child gratefully held her arms high to be picked up.

"Can Gail take me to the park today? I want to feed the pigeons."

"Didn't you do that yesterday?"

"They'll be hungry today, too."

Annabel squeezed her daughter and put her on the floor. "I thought you and Gail were going to the library today."

"We can go later. Can we go to the park?"

"I don't know."

"Gail said we might see her angel."

Annabel frowned. She would have to talk to Gail again. Gail was a wonderful nanny, but she needed to learn not to fill Shannon's mind with fanciful stories. Fairy tales were all right, and nursery rhymes.

Shannon enjoyed hearing about all kinds of fictional characters. She liked to have Gail read book after book from the library. But Gail talked about angels as though they were real. And Shannon believed anything Gail told her about angels.

"I'll talk to Gail," Annabel said. "Why don't you go to your playroom and Gail and I will work it out."

"OK—Kiss?" She raised on tiptoes and Annabel leaned down, taking a kiss on the cheek and giving one in return. Then Shannon ran out of the room.

Annabel frowned again. She really would have to be firm with Gail. She had tried to make clear to Gail that there was a difference between Shannon's being exposed to stories from books, and hearing talk about angels being real. The trouble was, Gail really believed in angels. She had her own angel, even had a name for it—April.

Gail had told her of first seeing April the night her mother died. Gail was a nanny in another family's home, living more than four hundred miles from her mother. And that night she had wakened up to find April standing at the foot of her bed. April told her of her mother's passing, but she said Gail should not be worried. Her mother was happy and wanted Gail to know that she loved Gail and would see her again one day. Gail was terrified of April, but then April faded from view. And suddenly Gail was no longer afraid. She felt a deep sense of peace.

The other time Gail had seen April was at the Bushingland Park. Gail was new to the city then, and was about to head down a certain path when she saw a woman sitting on a park bench. As Gail moved closer she recognized April. All April said was, "Not this path—that one." Something kept Gail from asking any questions, and she immediately turned to follow the new path. In a few moments Gail heard a faint voice calling from behind some bushes. Gail cautiously moved through the bushes and came upon an elderly woman who was lying next to her walking stick under an oak tree.

"I can't get up," the woman said. Gail reached down and took hold of the woman's arm. The woman struggled to rise. "I can walk if I can just get up."

"What were you doing so far off the path?" Gail asked.

"I saw a bird fly down from that tree like it was wounded or hurt. I wanted to see."

"Where is the bird?"

The woman shook her head. "It was on the ground. I thought it was injured. But when I reached down it flew right at my face. That's when I fell."

Gail walked with her to the path. "Are you all right now?"

"Yes. Thank you. I don't know what I would have done if you hadn't come by."

"Someone else would have come."

Annabel didn't believe in angels. She thought Gail had dreamed the first story. The second, well—she could have seen someone on a park bench who reminded her of April. Why that woman sent Gail to help rather than go herself, Annabel didn't know. But there are a lot of strange people in the city, and some would say Gail was strange. In fact, after the angel business came up, she and Fred had discussed whether Gail was suitable for Shannon after all.

But Gail was highly recommended by the three families she had worked for in other cities. Good nannies were always hard to find, and Shannon obviously liked Gail. What Gail believed about angels was really her own business. Other people believed in angels, too. But Annabel did insist that Gail not talk about angels anymore to Shannon. And Gail had seemingly followed that instruction, until today.

Gail was in the kitchen putting dishes into the cabinet.

"What's this about taking Shannon back to the park today?" Annabel asked.

"I was going to ask you about it."

"Shannon said you mentioned an angel."

"I'm sorry. It slipped out."

"You know how I feel about that kind of talk. Shannon's at a very impressionable age."

"Yes, Ma'am."

"And don't 'ma'am' me, Gail. I'm Annabel."

"Yes—Annabel."

Annabel smiled. "Of course you can go to the park, but I want her to get to the library."

"We will."

Driving to her store, Annabel rehearsed some of the thoughts she would give at the luncheon. She'd refer to her husband. Fred had already been well established in his career when they met. She had only been out of college a year, and with her best friend Gloria had sought a loan for starting a dress shop. They wanted to be partners, with Gloria sticking closer to the office and Annabel handling the public image challenge.

Fred had spotted her at the bank, taking a special interest in their request, and their relationship had progressed from there. On her part, what began as a professional interest rapidly changed to something more personal. Whirlwind courtship? Well, Fred's colleagues kidded him about being conservative in his business practices and something else in his courting procedures.

The fact is, Fred had admired her ambition, encouraged her in her plans, and counseled her and Gloria in the many details of starting their enterprise.

What she wouldn't tell the group was his present attitude.

"I don't think a nanny's the full solution," he had told her one night after finishing a six-ounce porterhouse steak at Canby's Squire Inn.

"What do you mean?"

He waited until he took a sip from his glass of Beaulieu's sauvignon blanc. "A little too fruity," he said. He looked from the glass and met her eyes.

"I think you should spend more time at home."

She put down her own glass and stared back. "I thought we were in agreement."

"We are. But things can change."

"Like what?"

He hesitated. "We're not getting younger. If we want another child—" He took another sip of wine. "It's just that—I talked to Candice today."

"Is she all right?" Annabel asked. "I talked to her yesterday."

"She wasn't feeling very well."

"She told me she was feeling a little better."

He shook his head. "Seems to be a daily thing. She's riding a roller coaster."

Annabel was silent. Candice was Fred's sister, who was trying to have another baby. She had miscarried last year, and was terrified she was going to lose this one. "Maybe we need to go see her," Annabel said.

"She told me it's helped her a lot, just being able

to talk to you. She's grateful for all your phone calls and the times you've dropped by."

"I wish I could do more."

"She's aware of her age. That scares her more than anything."

"The doctor reassured her—"

"I know, but she *is* thirty-seven."

She stared at him. "And you think we might be getting too old to have another baby?"

"No—"

"I'm thirty-two. We were only going to wait two more years."

"I know. It's just that—every year adds risk." He took another sip of his wine, and spoke softly. "I think we should try to have another baby now."

"I see."

He was exasperated. "We're just not getting any younger—either one of us."

"Fred, we talked about waiting two more years before another baby. You know I want to get the store expansion done first."

"There's another reason," Fred said. "I think Shannon needs a brother or sister before that."

"When did you get this revelation?"

"When we were interviewing nannies."

"You didn't say anything."

"You know how many nannies we looked at before we found Gail."

"We were lucky to find her."

"I know. But I started thinking about the way a nanny affects the life of the family. Anyone living in our home affects Shannon, and I know how I felt growing up with my sister. I want Shannon to have a brother or sister."

"So do I. We're only talking about two years. And having someone like Gail for a nanny makes that two years easier to accept."

"But Gail can't take the place of her mother," Fred said.

"What does that mean?"

"Having a baby is just part of what I've been thinking. I think you should ease off your work and stay home more."

"Am I hearing a hidden agenda?" she asked. Fred didn't reply.

Annabel looked away a moment and noticed two men standing by a woman seated at the bar, facing the dining area. One man was lighting a cigarette for the woman, and she was leaning forward more than she needed to, causing the man with the lighter no longer to be looking at her cigarette. Annabel gave a little sigh and looked back at her husband.

"We both wanted children," she said. "And when Shannon came I didn't ask you to give up your career."

"I'm not asking you to do that."

"But somehow I'm in a different category from you, isn't that it? The baby grew in me, but nine months of my unique focus on that child isn't enough. A child is born and a father and mother are both in place and positioned to rear it, but somehow parenthood isn't an equal opportunity vocation. The woman punches the time clock more often—that's what she's supposed to do, right?"

They stared at each other. Finally, his eyes dropped. "Let's talk another time."

"Let's talk now," she said, "because I think we're talking about something basic to our relationship. I thought we already had this worked out, but all of a sudden you're talking about making some rule changes."

"All right," he said, "I'll give my speech. I love you, and that means I love *you*. What you are. Your drive, your ambition, your talent, your career, your business ability—all of that is you. I want you to have your career, and I'm glad we have a nanny. With both of us working we need a nanny. But if you could spend just a little more time at home—Gail is great, but she's not you. If you could do that, and tried to get pregnant, well—it just seems a time to pull back from your work a little bit."

She looked at him reflectively. "All right, I'll consider it. I still remember the morning sickness from last time. And I remember how it felt when I got big. Gloria had to put in a lot of overtime running things. It would be harder this time, but at least I'll consider it."

"Good."

She grinned. "The store expansion and my expansion at the same time." Then she quit grinning. "But this idea that I can be more of a mother than I already am—I don't buy that. My career's as important to me as yours is to you. We can afford a nanny, and that lets us both work. To me, that's the way it ought to be."

As she drove downtown the memory of his smile warmed her heart. She pulled into the parking lot of the Gloria Annabel, Ltd. store. She always enjoyed seeing what dreams and hard work had created on this street corner. She and Gloria had long ago decided on the image they wanted to project for the store. Lettering simple and understated, fixtures at a minimum, colors muted, merchandise easy to reach yet displayed with elegance. They wanted to project quality beyond that of the typical department store, yet with popular pricing that would appeal to the middle class. The formula worked, and now they had leased the space in the adjoining building, and were planning to tear down the separating wall and expand their floor space.

Various customer representatives spoke to her as she moved toward the rear, where the offices were. Gloria was behind her desk talking on her phone. "We need that shipment by Tuesday, Mr. Waterbone. One hundred fifty, that's right. We're designing an ad for the next Sunday paper and we want to make sure we can have the coats on racks when the store opens Monday. All right. That's fine. Thanks."

Gloria hung up and smiled at Annabel. "Waterbone always runs tight."

"Sorry I'm a little late. I was rehearsing my speech for the women's club today, and then Gail and I had another discussion about angels."

"Is she still working out all right?"

"Perfectly. Sometimes she seems almost heaven-sent."

Gloria smiled. "Maybe she is, with her having her own angel."

"I know. Sounds strange. But she honestly believes that two times she's seen a real angel, one who talked to her."

"I wish angels *were* real," Gloria said. "Wouldn't it be great to know you had a guardian angel?"

"But the mystery would always be why some people see them and some don't."

"Maybe it's just a matter of faith," Gloria said.

"Maybe people can't see them because they simply don't believe they're real."

"You may be right. I know I've never seen one."

"Here's another thought. Maybe you personally don't need to see one. Maybe *you* don't need to have that much faith."

"What do you mean?"

"Gail believes she's seen one. She believes they're real. If she believes that strongly, maybe her faith can affect her angel or another angel to watch over you or Shannon."

"Well," said Annabel, "that's a new thought. And here's another new thought—I'd better get to work."

Shortly past noon Annabel was sitting at the head table looking out over a number of circular tables around which nearly one hundred fifty women were finishing their dessert after a meal of chicken á la king. She was more nervous than she expected to be. If she had a guardian angel, she hoped it would help her now.

She had long since quit eating, and was mentally rehearsing her speech while giving nodding recognition to the frequent comments of the club's president, who was sitting next to her. Finally the president stood and tapped on her glass. She made introductions of the guests seated at the head table, then turned to Annabel.

"I don't like long introductions, so I'll simply say that Annabel Overstreet is an ideal choice to speak on our subject today, 'How a Woman Can Have It All.' That subject title might seem idealistic or even egotistical. But I think that Annabel has demonstrated it's possible for a woman at least to come close to having it all. She has a career, a husband, and a child.

That means she's a businesswoman, a wife, and a mother. She's partner of Gloria Annabel, Ltd., and I imagine many of you today are wearing her clothes. Her husband is a vice president of the Merchant's Street National Bank. And her daughter is a lively three-year-old with the name of Shannon. So everyone please welcome Ms. Annabel Overstreet."

Annabel stood as the president sat. She positioned herself behind the microphone as the applause died down.

"Thank you Ms. President, honored guests, and all of you seated before me. Let me say first I don't think a woman should have it all, because after that nothing would happen. If you want a dozen apples and you pick a dozen apples, you have them all, then the picking stops. But a woman's existence never stops. It's true, I have a career and a husband and a daughter. But every day something forces me to realize I don't have it all. Something is always less than perfect. Something always needs to be done.

"And this is true for all of you. Each of you has a career. Some of you are married without children; others have children; some of you no longer have husbands or children. Regardless, all of you can come close to having it all as anyone else. Because having it all is a goal, not an accomplishment. When we make the best of what we have, do the best we know how, we are moving toward that goal.

"So what it comes down to is this—confidence, balance, and love . . ."

Annabel then spent time on each of these three points, referring to her personal experience: the confidence she felt when she wanted to start her own business; the balance she tries to maintain while performing as a business woman, wife, and mother; the love that doesn't stay within the walls of a home but extends in the degree of interest and concern she feels for employees and customers and all whose lives she touches.

Many women came to her afterward to express their appreciation. As she greeted the crowding well-wishers, one woman in her fifties pressed two tickets into her hand.

"Annabel, I want you to have these tickets for the Fun Fair next Saturday at Richland Mall. Bring your daughter. She'll love it. Food, games, rides—all on the parking lot."

Annabel smiled her thanks. Later in the car, before starting the engine, she glanced at the tickets and saw they were complimentary tickets to any two rides, offered in the name of Edna's Notions. Richland Mall was the city's largest mall, and the Fun Fair was an annual observance with an outside carnival furnishing the rides and games. Annabel mentally made plans to take Shannon.

The rest of the day was a series of phone calls, visiting with two manufacturer's reps who were referred to her by Gloria, counseling with an employee about a personal problem that was affecting job performance, talking to her window dresser about next month's displays and the need for some new mannequins, and moving around the floor talking to employees and customers. She tried not to think about the mess that would come when workers started knocking down the wall for the expansion.

Driving home, she realized that she still was unsettled about the baby question. She could have the baby now, but she could also wait two years as they had planned. Fred's opinion was important to her, but in the give-and-take of their marriage she felt that her opinion should be equally important. What was best for Shannon was certainly important. And the store and Gloria were important. Many factors to weigh and judge.

The first thing she did on reaching the house was to call Candice and make plans for her and Fred to visit Candice after dinner that night. Except for special occasions, Gail's responsibilities for Shannon ended when Annabel or Fred arrived home. Annabel loved to cook, and after getting dinner started she sat on the floor next to a dollhouse while Shannon busily moved people around. When Fred arrived she told him about going to Candice's house.

"I want you to do something with Henry while Candice and I talk."

"No problem," Fred said. "I'll get him to the pool table."

Annabel had never found it hard to talk to Candice, but on this night she sensed a tension under the surface, light talk covering up a secret dread. Henry seemed relieved when Fred suggested they play a game of pool. Annabel finished up the cup of coffee Candice had served.

"How have you been feeling today?" she asked. "Really."

"It doesn't get better—this feeling I have."

"Did you talk to the doctor?"

"Not today. He thinks I need a psychiatrist as it is."

"He's there to listen as much as to do something."

"He can't do anything. And I feel like I'm going to lose this baby no matter what I do."

"Candice, when you lost—the other baby, you said you had no warning?"

"I went to bed and I was asleep and I had a dream. I dreamed the doctor was delivering the baby. And I woke up, and—" her voice trailed off. She put her cup down on the coffee table. "The way I feel is not that something's wrong. I felt fine before, but feeling fine meant nothing. The fact that I'm feeling all right guarantees nothing now. Because it can happen without warning. And—" Candice's eyes moistened, "—I'm afraid, Annabel, I'm always afraid."

Annabel moved to her on the sofa and put her arms around her. For a few moments Candice cried softly, then she straightened. "We've always wanted children, and this may be our last chance. But I feel like no one can help."

Annabel thought for a moment. "You've met Gail, our nanny. She has an interesting idea, that people have angels that look after them."

"A guardian angel?"

"It's a comforting thought. If we knew we had an angel, then we could face almost anything, and we wouldn't be afraid."

"I wish I had an angel."

"Maybe you do."

"You don't believe that."

"Maybe I do. Gail believes she's seen one—twice. Both times the angel helped her, or helped someone through her."

After a moment Candice shook her head. "I can't believe that. Where was my angel when I lost my baby?"

"I don't know, but—" Annabel picked up Candice's hand, "—would you mind if I asked Gail to tell you firsthand her stories? They might help you."

Candice smiled. "All right. I'll listen, but I don't think any stories she tells could be of any help."

The next morning Annabel was about to leave the house when she turned back to Gail. "I meant to ask you something, Gail. You remember my sister-in-law, Candice Martin?"

"Yes. I dreamed about her last night."

"About Candice?"

"I'm supposed to tell you something that will help her."

"Come with me," Annabel said, leading Gail to two dining room chairs. "Tell me what you dreamed."

"I was going to tell you tonight." She hesitated. "I didn't dream of Candice, actually. I saw my angel. She said that Candice's baby would be all right."

Annabel tried to focus her thoughts. Gail had met Candice once. It had been obvious that Candice was pregnant. But Annabel had never talked about Candice, had never mentioned any possible problem about the baby.

"Is something wrong with the baby?" Gail asked.

"No." Annabel shook her head. "Not yet. But Candice had a miscarriage last time."

"Then you can tell her not to worry this time."

"*You* tell her, Gail. That's what I wanted to ask you. Would you talk to Candice and tell her about your angel visits? And now you have something even better to tell her."

"I'll be glad to talk to her."

"I'll phone and ask her if we can drop over tonight, if that's all right."

"Fine."

Annabel smiled and patted her shoulder and then stood. "I wish I could believe in angels like you do. I'm afraid I'd have to see an angel do something miraculous, something that could not be explained any other way."

Gail rose to stand beside her. "Angels can do anything, Annabel."

That night Candice had a lot of questions to ask Gail. Annabel couldn't tell how much, if any, of the stories Candice believed. But she could tell that Candice was affected by Gail's dream. She wanted desperately to believe the baby would be all right, and here was someone who dreamed of an angel giving that promise.

On Saturday Shannon was bubbling over in the car on the way to Richland Mall. She really didn't know what a carnival was, but she knew she was going to some place exciting with her mother. Fred was playing golf with two coworkers and an out-of-town bank official. Annabel was glad to have this time alone with Shannon, and she hadn't been to a carnival in years.

When they got to the mall it seemed like the whole parking area was filled with rides and tents. Fortunately, the mall had constructed a five-story concrete open parking facility on the north end. Otherwise, cars would have had to fight for limited parking spaces on nearby side streets.

Annabel pulled the car up the circular ramp deck after deck, moving slowly to look for a space. Finally she was on the top deck under open sky. She finally found a space at the far end near the exit drive.

I hope it's worth it, she thought, after she had unbuckled Shannon. Then, looking at Shannon jumping up and down with anticipation, she knew it was. They found the elevator and went down.

The two complimentary tickets from Edna's Notions were used for the merry-go-round and the teacup dip. These weren't enough for Shannon, of course, so Annabel purchased ten ride tickets and spent the next thirty minutes looking for rides that appealed to Shannon which weren't too grown-up. Shannon liked the pony ride. She also liked to watch people tossing rings at pegs and throwing balls at wooden milk bottles. The cotton candy was new to Shannon, and she wanted an ice-cream cone. They finished up on the Ferris wheel.

The carnival wasn't as big as the full-scale carnivals that used to fill the open fields near small towns all across the Midwest. But Shannon didn't know that, and her delight made the whole afternoon a rewarding time together.

Shannon reluctantly took Annabel's hand when it was time to make their way to the parking ramp. The elevator let them out on the top deck. The cars had thinned out. Some cars were pulling away. An engine was being gunned. Annabel looked in all directions as she led Shannon to the car. "Stay close to me," she said as she unlocked the door on Shannon's side, which was next to the exit drive. She was leaning in and separating the safety belt for Shannon when she heard the noise. An engine was roaring and growing louder. Tires squealed and a car rounded the curve nearest them and headed down their lane. Annabel looked back and was horrified. The car was headed straight toward them. Without thought she grabbed up Shannon, and knew the onrushing shape of red and chrome was the image of death.

She felt something just before she heard the crash, something solid under her arms. And then she was standing, tightly holding Shannon, fifteen feet on the other side of her car. A teenage boy was slumped over the steering wheel of the red car, not moving. Several people were rushing toward the accident.

"Are you all right?" a voice asked.

Annabel looked behind her and saw a man in his seventies. "I think so," she said.

The man's voice was shaking. "I saw the whole thing. He was coming right at you. I don't see how you moved that fast." Annabel stared at him. He shook his head. "I couldn't have moved that fast even when I was young. My eyes aren't as good as they used to be." He gave a nervous laugh. "My wife would laugh at me if I told her what I thought I saw."

"What?"

"It's silly."

"What did you see?"

He shook his head. "I thought . . ." He swallowed. "I thought I saw you fly over the car. I couldn't have, of course. So I know I didn't see you move. I just don't see how you moved that fast."

Annabel turned from him and hurried toward the cars. Two men were carefully helping the driver out, who was conscious and holding his head.

"Lucky he had his seat belt on," one man said.

Annabel saw the boy was no more than sixteen. "My head hurts," he mumbled, and Annabel knew he had been drinking. One of the men turned to Annabel. "You all right, ma'am?"

"Yes."

"I'll call the police." He turned and then looked back. "You're lucky. He came straight at you."

Annabel leaned back against a nearby car. "What happened, Mommy?" Shannon asked.

"You might not understand, Shannon—" Annabel was staring at a memory, a fleeting memory of two hands under her shoulders that lifted her and placed her gently on the ground fifteen feet away. "I don't understand," she said.

6

Ken's Angel

The angels of God are our angels, as Christ is God's and also ours

—AUGUSTINE

Ken Mullins had been waiting in the duck blind for two hours sixteen minutes and twenty-one seconds. He knew because he had put his Casio digital in stopwatch mode. He always did that. From the moment he waited at ready to the time the first bird fell—press button, bang, and stop the watch. Six years he had been keeping records, about as long as he had kept his daily jogging distances. He liked to keep records— jogging, swimming, bicycling, and how long it took him to bring down a bird. Records helped him keep going. His shortest time for a bird had been twenty-two seconds. The longest—today was the longest. He glanced at Chuck and Nell—the two Chessies were waiting patiently on the other side of Jeff. Then he shivered while breath poured from his mouth, making fog that would have clouded his aim, if he had needed to aim. What he needed was an extra handkerchief.

"Why do you have to go hunting today?" his wife had muttered from the bed. Hunting was the last thing she would ever do, unless hunting for an antique from the colonial period. "You know what the weatherman said," she added.

"It's *supposed* to be cold this time of year."

"At least take an extra handkerchief."

So he didn't. All he did was finish buttoning his coat and say, "What would happen if I stayed home and we tried to talk?" She stared at him and then turned her head away and leaned back on the pillow.

"Have fun," she said, closing her eyes.

Now he looked at the barrel of his Browning over-and-under. His father had given him this shotgun for his birthday, a thing of beauty and the pride of his father's extensive collection. He had always promised Ken this gun would one day be his.

Ken glanced at Jeff. "Maybe all the birds have already gone south."

Jeff grinned. "Patience, my boy. That's what I tell my salesmen. Patience will win."

"Yeah. The birds are in Cancun buying postcards to send north while we freeze."

Jeff owned a used car lot. They had been best friends since college. Suddenly Chuck and Nell grew restless. Ken strained to hear the sound he knew would be coming. Jeff nodded with satisfaction. "I told you. Patience."

Ken heard it then and shivered, but not from the cold. He listened as the sound grew ever louder—that multithroated babble that always sent a sharp thrill through his stomach. Voices—like children singing a nonsense song, ever louder—the traveling music of fast-flying geese, resonating in his heart.

He raised the Browning to his shoulder, squinting over the barrel as he saw the first line in V-formation move across the sky. The sound flooded around them as Jeff's gun fired first. Ken kept sighting along his barrel—leading, yes, leading—but not too much. A little less. Yes, that's it. Fire! The gun recoiled against his shoulder. The other barrel—*fire*. Then Ken's heart bounded as he saw two birds spiraling down toward the water. Jeff fired three more times with his pump-action Remington as Chuck and Nell hit the water and began swimming with strong leg action. Ken stopped his watch and looked at Jeff.

"Two," he said.

Jeff held up one finger and shook his head. "I should have brought Betsy." Betsy was a Remington double-barrel Jeff had owned for eleven years. "Sam here had better shape up." Jeff put more shells into the pump-action shotgun. Ken reloaded his own gun and watched with admiration the work of the dogs. Swimming proudly and smoothly, they reached the shore and held the birds gently until releasing them to outstretched hands.

Another hour passed. Then two. No further flights. Ken looked at Jeff who returned the look with a shrug. With unspoken consent both began preparations to leave. By this time Ken was so numb he couldn't feel the cold. Martha had never understood his passion for hunting. He had explained how his father had taken him hunting as a child. He had tried to describe the open-eyed wonder of a ten-year-old boy tramping through the fields with a dad and a dog, seeing the world as a wonderland of adventure. She couldn't comprehend how, after all these years, the lure of the hunt still held him with unfailing anticipation.

Probably she was relieved that they had no sons he could instill with the same interest. Both daughters left the outdoors strictly to him. Fifteen-year-old Ellen had never wanted to go hunting with him, and now was more interested in boys than anything else. But eleven-year-old Susan—he had hoped Susan might come to share in the same joy he felt for the hunt. She had always been an active child, full of laughter and energy. One time she had gone with him to a quail ranch, trying to be enthusiastic, to be what he wanted. But when she saw the first bird fall, and looked at that dead bird in her father's hand, she had cried. The hunt ended right there, along with any hope of sharing this part of his life with a child. "Daddy," she had said, "God doesn't want you to kill animals."

Riding back to town in Jeff's Jeep Cherokee, the dogs moving restlessly behind them, Ken reflected on how many times Susan and Martha let "God" carry the weight of any argument. As far as hunting was concerned, Ken could refer to Genesis, where God said man would have dominion over all the animals, and how every living creature would be food for him. Not good enough.

Ken turned to Jeff. "You ever have any trouble talking to Kathy?"

"Not lately," Jeff smiled.

"You talk much about religion?"

"You know how active she is at church."

"I don't mean that. Do you talk about your beliefs?"

Jeff shook his head. "Not much. When we married that was our understanding. We think differently about religion and politics. I attend church, but Kathy's always been a lot more active than I."

"Does she see God doing everything—like what happens is always God's will?"

"No." Jeff glanced at Ken. "You having a problem?"

Ken nodded. "Maybe. Martha's almost a fanatic, at least about some things. And she's influenced Susan."

They rode in silence. Finally Ken spoke again. "We've been married a long time. But the last couple of years—I don't know. We don't talk, don't communicate. Except for the kids, we don't have any common interests. And then this thing about religion—it's got worse since her mother died."

"Have you talked to your pastor?"

"I've thought about it. But what's he going to say? Religion is what his life is all about."

"Maybe professional counseling?"

"I've never wanted to think we needed that, but I don't like what's happening. We don't have much of a marriage anymore. We're like strangers living in the same house." Ken hesitated, then straightened up and looked at Jeff. "Hey—I'm sorry. Forget I said that."

"We're friends, aren't we?"

"Sure."

"And friends can talk."

"But you don't need to hear this. I've tried to talk to Martha, but she looks at me like I'm crazy. Then she gets angry, and brings 'God' into it, or maybe an angel."

"An angel?"

"She's got a guardian angel. Says everyone has. And Susan believes it."

Jeff turned left on a tree-lined street and then slowed down to pull into the driveway of the third house from the corner. Shrubs bordered the property line until reaching the front of a two-car garage connected by a breezeway to a Southern colonial–style house.

"Let's leave the dogs at home and go out Friday for quail," Ken said.

"Are you kidding? We won't get any quail without dogs."

"We'll make noise, kick up a fuss, flush them out."

"They'll hide and walk away without a dog to spook them. We'll never see any."

"So it's more difficult. Be a good change from a duck blind."

Jeff shook his head. "I can't Friday, anyway. Got an auction in Atlanta. Some of us have to work."

Ken smiled. "I'll admit it's been easier since I brought my nephew into the operation. OK—I'll hit it alone."

"Sure you don't want the dogs?"

"Not this time."

"Maybe your guardian angel will flush out the quail. Hey—I'm sorry." Jeff was grinning. Ken waved him off and turned toward the house.

Inside Susan was parked on a chair in the kitchen talking on the phone and eating a sausage biscuit at the same time. She looked up. "Mom went to the Home Show with Edna." Ken remembered Martha's mentioning this at dinner last night. As he moved into the den he heard Susan's voice back on the phone, ". . . and the dream was really beautiful. I mean the angel was dressed in a golden robe and he looked straight at me . . ."

Ellen was in the den watching a Saturday morning comedy sitcom—rerun, of course. "Hi, Dad," she said.

"How about going with me to the Home Show after I shower?"

"Mom's gone there."

"I know."

"She said you didn't want to go."

"Changed my mind. Anyway, you know we've been talking about remodeling the kitchen."

Ellen looked perplexed. "I don't like to go to those things."

"Just the two of us. Maybe we'll get some ideas."

"I'm supposed to meet Marilyn this afternoon, to study for our history test."

"OK. Good idea." He turned and walked back through the kitchen as Susan put down the phone.

"What's this about a dream?" he asked.

"The same dream again. I've told you about it."

"You saw an angel?"

"Right. And he told me to persevere."

"Persevere?"

"Never give up. To keep trying."

"Trying what?"

"I've told you before. To try and find the truth."

"The truth about what?"

"I don't know. About everything, I guess. To seek the truth about everything."

"Why can't the angel be more specific?"

Susan was exasperated. "That would spoil everything. I mean, all of life. That's what I need to find out. Not one specific thing."

"I see." Ken nodded. "Makes sense." He started to walk away."

"Dad," Susan said. He turned back to her. "Are you and Mom having problems?"

"Why do you ask that?"

"Just a feeling. You don't seem to talk to each other much anymore."

"We'll be OK," he told her.

"The angel said something."

"What?"

"He said you needed to find the truth."

Ken stared at her. "The angel talked about me?"

"He said two people I love needed to know the truth."

"That's all he said?"

Susan nodded. "I know he was talking about you and Mom."

He paused again. "Well, truth is important," he said.

After showering, he decided against the Home Show, and drove down to his office instead. He pulled into a fenced lot past a sign that said "Mullins Trucking." A guard waved at him. "Good afternoon, Mr. Mullins."

"Hello, Jimmy. How's it going?"

"Quiet, Mr. Mullins. But Mr. Carew is here."

His nephew. He often pleaded with Bill to stay away from the office on Saturdays. But Bill was a workaholic, and Ken has to admit his own duties were easier with Bill on board. He was lucky. Bill had been looking for a change after eleven years with a brick manufacturing firm. He was a skilled project manager, and Ken needed help for a business that had grown rapidly over the past five years.

Hiring a relative was something Ken considered carefully. But Bill was only five years younger than himself, the son of Ken's much older half sister. Combined with his maturity, Bill had an excellent work record, and Ken soon found he had made an outstanding choice. They not only worked well together, but had developed a closeness that extended beyond formal ties. Ken knew he was lucky to have not one, but two close friends.

Bill was sitting at the computer when Ken stuck his head in. "Hi, Bill."

Looking up. "Ken—how was hunting?"

"Got two. Everything OK?"

"Just finishing up this Gantt timeline. Didn't expect to see you here."

"You ought to take off and go hunting with me sometime."

"That outdoor stuff isn't for me."

"That's what you say. But you could build hunting into a Gantt chart."

Bill shook his head. "I'll stick to hunting for new business."

Ken hesitated. "If you're almost finished, do you think we could talk?"

"Sure."

"Not about business."

Bill pulled back from the computer and leaned back. "Have a chair."

Ken sat and hesitated again. "You remember one time when we were talking about kids, and you said your daughter kept your marriage together through one rough spot?"

"I remember."

"You said you and Joan weren't seeing things the same way."

Bill nodded. "We were arguing all the time. We couldn't agree on anything. The wallpaper pattern, for goodness' sake. What movie to see. The color of the new car."

"And you thought of divorce?"

"Only Kate kept us together. That little three-year-old girl was like an angel sent from God. We had tried for years to have a child. Given up hope. Then Kate came. An angel."

Ken grinned. "That's one thing I wanted to talk about."

"Kate?"

"Angels."

Bill stared at him. Ken asked, "Do you believe in angels?"

Bill didn't answer and Ken continued. "I don't mean in the figurative sense. Your daughter's an angel, all right. But I mean—real angels."

"I've never seen any."

"People have—some people. My daughter says an angel appears to her in dreams. My wife believes she has a guardian angel and talks to him like I'm talking to you."

"Interesting."

"That's one word for it."

"I believe angels might be real. Just because I haven't seen one doesn't mean anything."

"Angels are just part of it. Martha believes in angels and I don't. But that's just one thing we don't agree on. We used to argue, too, like you and Joan did, over everything. So now we don't argue; we don't talk. We don't communicate, period."

"Just a minute." Bill bent over the keyboard and closed out the program, turning off the computer. Then he pushed back in his chair and propped his feet on the desk. "OK. I knew there was a reason I needed to come in today. I just didn't know the real one."

"I shouldn't take your time with this."

"We've both got the time now. Let's talk it out."

"I think we've about covered it," Ken said, "but I don't know what to do."

"When did things begin to go wrong?"

"Martha and I never had a lot in common. Not many outside interests, but she seemed interested in me. And in the early years that was enough. Then the kids came and we had that. But the kids aren't babies anymore."

"And you're in your middle years."

"What do you mean?"

"Mid-life crisis."

"You think it's my fault?"

"Whoa," Bill said. "Not anybody's fault. Just a fact of life."

"I'm not ogling the twenty-something females."

"Look, I'm in *my* mid-life crisis, and I'm not chasing women. But I am more restless than I used to be. I'm aware I'm not as young, that I've got less hair, that I can't run as fast or jump as high. And I don't like it. I always want to show I'm not getting older, that I'm as good or better than I ever was. And there are many ways to try and prove it besides having affairs with younger women. I mean, why do I work as much as I do?"

Ken smiled. "You're a workaholic?"

"Right. And you like to hunt. I know I've got a problem, but I'm dealing with it." Bill shrugged and spoke drily. "At least I'm not working on Sundays anymore." Hesitating. "Usually."

"So what's the answer?"

"First, recognition. The problem is not in the stars, Brutus—"

"But in myself."

"And then communication. Martha's a part of the situation, so you have to tell her how you feel."

"I don't know about that."

"Try to get hold of those original feelings again about Martha. A lot of the things you argue about might seem less important."

Ken slowly nodded. "Everything you say makes sense. But I don't like thinking this is all my fault."

"Martha's at fault, too. You both argue. You both have stopped talking to each other."

Ken grinned wryly. "But I think I'm the one who will have to start talking first."

"Just don't expect a miracle. Relationships take time to grow back."

Driving home, Ken tried to remember the first time he had seen Martha. He had been a college sopho-more sitting on a low wall outside the student center. He was reading Wordsworth in his English lit text-book when this gorgeous blond walked by. He barely saw her in profile before she was by. Without thought he stood and stared after her. Then he ran after her.

"Excuse me," he said, trying not to show he was breathing hard. "Did you drop this?" He held out a quarter. She looked at his hand and then at his face.

"No."

"How about this?" He held out a comb. She shook her head.

"Then how about telling me your name? I may find something else."

She said nothing.

"Phone number?" he asked. She still said nothing, and he began to grow uncomfortable in the extreme. "My mistake," he said, and started to leave.

"I've lost a turquoise earring," she said. He turned back, his smile victory incarnate. "My name is Martha Carroway, if you find it. I'm in Blackstone Dorm." She turned and walked away.

He didn't bother looking for any earring. But he did go to a jewelry store and buy two turquoise earrings.

That had been the beginning. And he wasn't worried then about common interests or communication. Something more important had sparked between them. Maybe the same spark could flame again if they both tried to find it together.

That night at dinner he tried to keep a light conversation going. Ellen was willing—she was always willing to talk. But Susan ate quietly, glancing occasionally at her mother. Martha spent time describing the Home Show.

Afterward the two girls loaded the dishes in the dishwasher as Ken motioned to Martha. "Let's go for a ride."

She looked puzzled. "Come on," he said.

He drove the car to Cawther's Park, to a place that overlooked city lights. Two other cars were parked nearby.

"Why did you bring me here?" she asked.

"Don't you know?" He took her left hand and touched the rings. She moved her hand away.

"Why are you doing this?"

"Seventeen years ago you knew."

"We're not the same people."

"You were wearing a purple suit with a white blouse that had red polka dots. And your hair was a ponytail with bangs that touched your eyebrows."

"Ken, don't—"

"Are you afraid to remember? Remember how we felt? I thought you were the most beautiful woman I had ever seen. My heart was beating so fast I was afraid you'd hear it. And when I put the ring on your finger I felt like emperor of the universe."

She said nothing, and he felt closer to her in this silence than he had in many months of halting conversations and angry words. The silence stretched and he felt he was walking beside her along an almost forgotten pathway. She turned to him then.

"Can it really have been seventeen years?"

He took her hand again, massaging the rings. "Proposing to you was the most important thing I ever did. It still is."

"Then what's happened? Why aren't we able to talk? Why are we living separate lives under one roof?"

"Maybe your guardian angel let us down," he said drily.

"Ken—" her voice reproached him.

"Sorry," he said. "Maybe he didn't let us down. Maybe I let him down. But isn't an angel supposed to be helpful? Why can't I see him, or dream about him? Or if I have my own angel, where is he?"

"Don't blame an angel for what's wrong in our marriage."

"Right. Someone reminded me that any fault is within ourselves. But you see my point here. I love you, but I can't think the way you do about everything. Angels are just an example."

"I've never insisted on that. But I do want you to accept what I believe as something I'm sincere about. And if you can't agree with me, at least you can—respect—my beliefs."

"I can do that."

"I've felt you were laughing at me."

"I never meant to hurt your feelings."

They stared at each for a long moment. Then their faces moved closer together and suddenly Ken knew another great truth—the spark was still there.

On Friday morning the alarm radio woke Ken up at five o'clock. The announcer gave the temperature as a crisp thirty-seven degrees—not too cold—just right for hiking through woods and fields. Charly Keller's farm was twenty miles north of town on State Highway 27. Charly bought his pickup trucks and sundry used cars from Jeff, and always welcomed Jeff and Ken to hunt his fields. Ken had called ahead so Charly would expect him.

The atmosphere in the Mullins's home was greatly improved. Martha still wouldn't go hunting with him, of course. And he didn't want to go scavenging antique stores with Martha. But they were talking, and making plans to compromise on events where both could attend. The symphony orchestra for him, a local college basketball game for her.

Dating again. How about that?

So if they didn't talk about angels, or argue politics

or religion—what could go wrong? Ellen eloping? Susan preaching on a street corner? Worry not. The future can hang itself, or go dancing down the boulevard of lost causes, or fly with eagles.

Ken decided on his old faithful Remington double-barrel twelve-gauge for the quail. He knew he might as well leave the gun behind, without a dog. But carrying the gun was almost as comforting as shooting it. And besides, maybe his own angel would have mercy and flush a bird. Martha sleepily muttered "Be careful" when he left.

He pulled his car to a stop in front of the Keller farmhouse. The clapboard was weathered gray and had a tin roof. A child's voice yelled from the house and the front door burst open. Roger Keller, eight years old, came rushing out. "You gonna hunt? Can I go with you?"

"Roger!" Charly Keller yelled. "Get back in here!" Charly came out the door and grabbed Roger's shoulder. "You haven't got your coat on. Now get back in there."

The boy reluctantly moved toward the house. "Can I go?"

"Not this time," Ken said.

Charly shook Ken's hand. "That boy has too much energy."

"Just wait till he gets older."

"Does it get easier?"

"Afraid not."

Charly gestured toward the east. "You've got it to yourself today. Jeff couldn't come?"

"An auction in Atlanta."

"I've been thinking about getting another truck.

Hope he finds some down there. Want some coffee before you go?"

Ken shook his head.

"Well, there'll be some when you get back. Doesn't seem too cold, but it's the kind that seeps into the bone. You'll be wanting some."

Ken waved and started walking. Soon the farm-house stood small against the shelter of trees. Then down a slope and the house was gone. The rutted field contained stubble and weeds and fallen limbs and trunks. He whistled "Old Macdonald," keeping his eyes going back and forth like an intermittent windshield wiper. *Bird, bird, fly up high. Flap your wings and say good-bye.*

He didn't expect to see any birds, but it was fun looking. And it was fun just walking in a world where the soul could expand beyond the tree line to the distant horizon. He walked for forty minutes, then an hour—seeing no living creature. He alternated crossing fields and woods. He knew he was outside Charly's property, but the land was not posted. Still, it was time to start back.

In a patch of woods he stopped. A large tree trunk lay on the ground, and sticking straight up was a limb two inches in diameter. He slowly lifted his gun and sighted toward the base. He squeezed a shot and the limb exploded from the trunk.

No quail had better try to pass me today, he thought, moving on. Through another patch of open ground, then more woods. Charly was right. He *was* getting cold. He stepped on a branch and suddenly a shape launched from a limb above him. He looked hastily up—a squirrel. At least something was out here. He came to another large tree trunk. An urge hit

him and he was ten years old again. He climbed upon
the trunk, balancing himself with the gun in one hand
and his empty arm on the other side. He walked its
length, and then slowly, carefully, he began to back
up. His right foot was inching back when he heard a
sound much louder than any squirrel. He turned, startled, and momentarily saw the tail end of a deer
bounding away. He was off-balance and started to
fall. The gun hit a piece of a limb and twisted; Ken
let it go and grabbed at another limb, missing. The
gun discharged right before he hit the ground.

He lay for a moment, stunned. And then his hand
felt wet. He was surprised to see it red. He was
bleeding! Now he felt the pain in his upper thigh. He
tried to stand up and crumpled back, nearly passing
out. He stayed that way for a long time. He knew he
had to make another effort. No one was around to
help him. Eventually Charly would come looking for
him. But he could bleed to death. He had to get up.
Stupid, stupid, stupid. He had violated a basic safety
rule. Keep the gun on safety. But he had fired one
shot and forgotten the safety. Great. But this wasn't
helping him get back. Up—try it again.

He made it to his feet this time and stood wob-
bling. He used the gun for a crutch and began slowly
shuffling forward. Out of the woods finally. Open
field finally. Painful, worse each step. And then more
woods. He knew then he wasn't going to make it.
And if Charly found him, it might be too late. But he
couldn't walk any farther. He couldn't limp, crawl,
swim, or fly another inch. He stood wavering, knowing he would fall in another moment. Then suddenly
he felt it, strength he didn't know he had. He took a
step, *and moved!* Another step—he could walk! He

couldn't believe it. He was walking. The pain was much less, and he could walk.

He walked for what seemed like hours until he saw the familiar farmhouse. And he could still walk, almost without pain. Finally he reached the front porch, and knocked on the door. Eight-year-old Roger saw him first. Then he froze.

"I've been shot," Ken said. Still Roger stood there staring. "Is your dad here?"

"Get him away!" Roger shouted.

"What?"

"He scares me. Get him away!"

At that moment Charly came up behind Roger. Seeing the blood, he yelled for his wife. Then he pushed open the door as Ken collapsed into his arms.

When Ken opened his eyes he was lying on a couch. "We got the bleeding stopped," Charly said, "but we need to get you to the hospital."

"What happened?"

"You passed out."

"I don't know how I made it back."

"That guy was holding you up," Roger said. Ken could barely see him behind his father.

"What guy? What are you talking about?"

"Hush, Roger," Charly said. "Your mother and I didn't see anyone."

"He was there."

"Who was there?" Ken asked.

"That glowing guy," Roger said. "He was scary. He had his arm around you."

"I said enough, Roger," Charly broke in. "No one was there."

"There was. He was dressed in white and glowing and then he disappeared when you opened the door."

Ken weakly grasped Charly's arm. "I think Roger's right. I didn't see him, but I felt him. I couldn't have made it without him. He carried me." He sat up slowly. "Let's get to the hospital."

Charly helped him to his feet, supporting his weight by holding him behind the back. "That's what the angel did," Ken said. "He supported me like this. But he was stronger than you." He looked at Roger. "You're lucky. You got to see him."

"He's scary."

"And we're probably scary to him," Ken said.

Riding in the car to the hospital one thought kept repeating itself to Ken—"Now Martha and I have got something new to talk about."

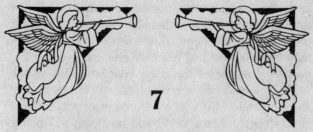

7

Randy's Angel

Each man has a guardian angel appointed to him

—AQUINAS

The pavement was still a little wet from the early morning frost. This was the best time for running, when dawn's light was still golden and the air was fresh as a new baby's outlook. One advantage of his job at the fire hall was the rotation schedule that gave him opportunity for long extended runs on days off. Of course, one disadvantage of that job was its contribution to the breakup of his marriage.

Randy Stewart didn't like thinking about that, but running the 11.2 miles through Macon Jones Park gave him lots of time to think about a lot of things. Jackie was one of them.

Looking back, he was always amazed that he had married Jackie Larson. They seemed a mismatch from the start. He was just out of the marines, taking a civil service exam, when he noticed this beautiful redhead sitting two rows ahead of him. He had never been shy, and after papers were handed in he managed to bump into her shoulder as she was about to pass through the door. That was six years ago, and their combination had been volatile and irresistible— another example of the adage that opposites attract.

He was outdoors; she was indoors. He was boxing; she was ballet. He was MTV; she was public television. He was cheeseburger and beer; she was porterhouse and wine.

His first date with her had been a movie—neutral ground. But from that point on their nights were a back-and-forth balance between two different worlds. She took him to his first symphony. He took her to her first roller-skating attempt. He had the most fun that night because he was always needing to touch her—lifting and supporting. But she was always a good sport and he was likewise, and each tried to appreciate and accept the appeal of strange activities.

One area never required any adjustment, however— the afterwards of all their dates that made both of them breathless in the closeness and touch and caress of fingers to skin and lips to lips. The chemistry between them was always a potential earthquake, and on some occasions became one.

After one such time, when the reclining seat turned his car into a Kublai Khan pleasure dome and they both lay quivering in each other's arms, Randy had asked the age old question and Jackie, as though swept by some elemental current she could not control, said yes.

By this time Randy had won placement with the city as a fire fighter. And Jackie—not accepting placement based on the civil service exam—entered

the secretarial pool at the Atkins, Graves, Littlefield
and Associates law firm.

If anyone had any doubts about their union, it was
Eldon Boles. Eldon had grown up with Randy. They
had separated after high school when Randy went
into the service. By the time Randy got back home
Eldon was married with one child and another on the
way. Now Ken Boles was eight, and Jan Boles was
six.

When Randy had asked Eldon to be his best man,
Eldon accepted, but he used that occasion to raise
some questions. He referred to his own relationship
with his wife Gladys. They liked the same things,
thought the same way on many issues, shared a
trunkload of common interests. Was Randy certain?

Had Randy possessed any such doubts, they would
have been greatly diluted by the influence of someone else—his future mother-in-law. Rebecca Larson
was a widow with three daughters—Jackie being the
youngest. The other two daughters were married and
living in other states. Rebecca and Randy had immediately bonded at some psychic level. Randy's own
parents were dead, and Rebecca became a second
mother. And on Rebecca's part, the feeling of kinship
was just as strong. She had never had a son. Two
sons-in-law, but she didn't feel as close to them as to
this thoughtful and humorous young man who obviously adored her daughter.

He and her daughter were different. She could see
that. But she also knew that her daughter was fortunate to have such a kind and considerate man in love
with her. Her words of encouragement were strategic
thrusts to promote harmony during the courtship. The
one big worry was Jackie's acquisitive nature. Re-

becca had learned long ago that qualities of personality were far more important than the accumulation of wealth. But Jackie liked material things; she liked money. And while his work was laudatory and worthwhile, Randy did not appear to have strong prospects for becoming rich. Rebecca longed for her daughter to grow up in every way, to be mature enough to understand what truly was important in relationships.

The end came not with a blowup. Alienation had become a habit that built a common resignation to what had to be. After dinner one night—his favorite dish, a seven-layer casserole Jackie had learned from her mother—she simply announced, "I'm leaving."

He tried to act surprised and hurt. He owed it to her to look chagrined and regretful and sorrowful. Actually, he was relieved. He was determined that they remain friends, and that no bitterness be part of the divorce. They sold the house and divided all assets, including the recent inheritance from his aunt in St. Louis. Aunt Gertrude had been his mother's only sister. She had never married, lived frugally, and saved a surprising amount of money during her many years of selling real estate.

Since no children were at issue, and because of her recent promotion as administrative assistant to one of the general partners, Jackie did not ask for alimony. Randy learned later that she might already have been thinking of a second marriage, to one of the firm's junior partners. She was now engaged.

But none of this changed his relationship to Rebecca. She was still his second mother, and he did not want anything to change that relationship. If he ever got married again, he knew she would be happy for him in the same way as any mother.

Not that he was thinking of marriage. He was not even dating anyone regularly. For six months after the divorce, he had no interest in dating anyone. But these last few months—well, he had begun to notice that some women looked pretty good. One thing he knew—love couldn't be rushed. And not even racing hormones would make him start looking at engagement rings. Marriage had to be based on more than sexual attraction. He had experienced the ultimate in that direction, and doubted if he would ever feel the same chemistry with any woman again.

The route through Macon Jones Park took him on a blacktopped road that rose up hills, crested on plateaus, and then dipped down to twisting turns and curves ranging from slight direction changes to radical switchbacks forced by U-turns. An annual marathon was held on this course by having runners complete two circuits plus a length of the boulevard that connected the park to the city. The course had come to be called "The Monster" by novice and experienced runners alike.

Randy loved it. One circuit of 11.2 miles bored out the arteries, toughened the heart, strengthened the ligaments, toned the muscles, and created a flood of endorphins that relieved tension and gave him a sense of well-being. The trouble was that most people wanted these results before they reached the appropriate level of fitness. Building fitness required time and patience, and anyone overrunning while underfit could damage the body and set up a conditioning that forever after associated physical effort with pain and discomfort. Randy had learned that the hard way, running too fast over too great a distance until he developed plantar fasciitis, a nagging heel injury that kept him from running for two months.

But now running was fun again. As he moved through the park he continually monitored his body to make sure that everything felt right, and was careful not to run too fast.

Markers were set up beside the road at each mile. When he moved past the seven-mile marker he started a long climb around a curve that ended with the road running parallel and above the steeplechase grounds. This was always one of his favorite scenes. Stretched out below him was a large field of jumps and water barriers for the horses. But times when there were no horses, runners would sometimes enter the field and run around the circumference. One circuit around equaled about a mile. It was a good run, and Randy had tried it once. But he seldom went down there because there were four miles still ahead of him to the park entrance where he was parked.

He saw no horses today, and continued to scan the field as he ran parallel to it. He was about to pass the field when he thought he saw someone—not moving, sitting? He wasn't sure, but then he saw the figure struggle up, and then fall back down into a sitting position. Randy stopped running. He squinted, hand shading his eyes, then began to run downhill. The ground was uneven and he watched to make certain of his footing.

He reached the bottom and could make out a woman. She was trying to stand again. He continued to run toward her, and details grew clearer with each step. Blue jogging jacket and pants. Long blond hair fastened behind her head and then flowing free in a ponytail reaching her shoulder blades. She looked backward and saw him and then he was standing beside her.

"My ankle—" she said, "please help me up." She held out her hand which he took, and she pulled herself up to stand on one leg. "I didn't see that hole."

He was surprised at her height. He was six feet one inch and her eyes were level with his. They were a dark shade of blue.

"Should you be standing?" he asked.

"It isn't broken. I'm a nurse, and I know that much." She tried to take a step and winced, holding her foot off the ground.

"You have a car?" he asked.

"I parked at Indian Springs. I was running on the road and when I saw the steeplechase field it looked so inviting I decided to make a circuit of it." She raised her eyebrows and grimaced. "I guess I should have left the field for the horses."

"That's the one problem with running down here— the horses have made mincemeat of some sections of ground. It's still a great run, though."

"But maybe not when you're alone," she said.

"Are you sure you can walk?"

She smiled. "No."

"Do you mind doing that again?" he asked.

"What?"

"Smile."

She looked at him quizzically. Then she held out her hand. "My name is Dani Kendrick."

He shook her hand. "I'm Randy Stewart."

"Do you happen to be parked anywhere near here?" she asked.

He shook his head. "At the park entrance."

"Then what if I gave you my keys. Indian Springs is only a mile from here and you could drive back."

"I've got a better idea," he said.

"What's that?"

"I could carry you to Indian Springs."

That smile again. "You're kidding—"

"Just think of me as your personal horse."

"You may not have noticed, Mr. Stewart, but I'm not exactly a small woman."

"You're tall," he said, "but I bet you don't weigh more than 140."

She nodded. "Close enough."

"I'm used to lifting weights a lot heavier than that, and please call me Randy."

She stared at him for a moment. "All right, Randy. You can be my horse. Just let me know when you want to stop and rest."

He turned his back and bent forward. She hitched herself up and he was holding both her legs under her knees.

"A little higher," he said, and she adjusted her weight upward. Once a week he went maximum on deep knee squats. The weight he balanced on his back with five reps was 410 pounds. Dani was a feather.

She marveled at his ease in climbing the hill. His back was tight, and his shoulders where her hands rested were hard and rounded and she had a sudden vision of the blacksmith in Longfellow's poem. She was tempted to let her hands slide down his arms and feel his biceps, but she kept her eyes focused on the road ahead. He was good-looking, though. *And he liked to run.* Darrell would never run, not even with her. She sighed. It would be nice to have a man as a running partner. She ran early mornings in her neighborhood before she had to go to the hospital, and on her days off she liked to explore different parts of the city for an extended run.

It would be nice to be able to run with someone, he thought. Particularly a woman. Particularly this woman. None of the guys at the fire hall were runners. They laughed at him for being a fitness fanatic. But they didn't laugh with a mean attitude. They had seen him do fifteen one-arm pushups with either arm. They had seen him chin himself three times using only one arm, the other arm held behind his back. They had seen him lift the bench table where they ate their meals, by gripping one table leg with one hand, and raising it straight out at shoulder height, holding it for five seconds. None of these things had been his idea, but came from verbal challenges that caused sides to be taken and bets made.

Randy had never dated a girl as tall as he. He imagined what it would be like on a date when she wore high heels, and he had to look up at her when he talked.

Looking up at a woman! Jackie was only five-four, petite in every way except for her voice, which was not petite.

They reached Indian Springs, a picnic area in the park comprising seven sheltered tables and cooking grills. Her car was parked beside one shelter. She had taste. It was a BMW 318i.

"Not a new one," she said when he complimented her. She stood awkwardly by the car, balancing on one leg as she unlocked the door. Then she turned to him. "Thank you. I don't know what I would have done if you hadn't come by."

"Next time why don't we start out together?" he said.

"I'm afraid it will be a while before my ankle is healed." She smiled.

"You said you're a nurse?" he asked.

She nodded, "At Good Samaritan Hospital."

"I work at the Macklin Village Fire Station."

"So you're a fire fighter?"

He nodded. "I do other things, too, like go to movies, roller skate, eat out. All of which I'd like to do with you."

"I see," she said. "How good are you at remembering?"

"I read poetry and can recite 'The Raven.' "

"Very impressive." She smiled and the sun was brighter. "But can you remember phone numbers?"

"Try me."

"832-5739."

"Got it," he said.

"I'll be home this afternoon." She got into her car and started the engine. "Thanks again for being my horse," she said, waving as the car sped away.

When he pulled into his driveway at home he saw Ruby Puckett next door mowing her front yard. Her three-year-old daughter Marie was standing in a playpen and waving at him as he got out of the car. He walked over to the playpen.

"Hi, Marie."

"Hi, Mr. Suwar," she said. She was jumping up and down and holding up a small rubber ball toward him. Randy reached out his hand and she dropped the ball. He reached down and grabbed it.

"You want to catch it?" he asked.

"Yes."

He lightly tossed it and she held out a hand, which the ball promptly hit and fell to the floor of the play-pen. She picked it up and held it out again. Randy looked at Ruby.

"She's going to be a ball player."

Ruby smiled, cutting off the motor and moving toward him. "You should feel honored. She doesn't play catch with everybody."

Randy took the ball and tossed it again. Marie's hand came up and this time the ball didn't make contact before hitting the floor.

"You have a good run?" Ruby asked.

"Better than usual," Randy said. "Mind if I pick her up?"

Ruby shook her head, and Randy reached and lifted Marie out of the playpen. He held her close and she jiggled up and down, putting her arms around his neck. The best feeling in the world, he thought. He wanted children someday. Maybe if he and Jackie had had children—

He had wanted to try, but Jackie wasn't ready. She must have had more sense than he, because the way things turned out not having kids was a blessing. He knew children wouldn't have saved their marriage. And using children as a means of keeping two people together was the worst possible solution for both the parents and offspring.

But he did want children. He wanted someone like Marie, whom he could pick up and hold close and who would put two small arms around his neck and greet his cheek with a juicy kiss. He had only been in this house five months since the divorce settlement and selling the other house, but he already loved this little girl who waved and smiled and wiggled with pleasure whenever she saw him.

Wiley and Ruby Puckett were both elementary school teachers. Ruby had taken leave from teaching. They were having a financial strain, but both felt that Ruby should be home until Marie was old enough for kindergarten. A four-foot-high wooden fence protected their backyard, allowing Marie freedom to play and at the same time keeping their dalmatian from roaming the neighborhood.

Wiley laughed when they realized that Randy was a fireman. "You're the one who should have Freckles."

One day Randy had borrowed Freckles to take him to the fire station. The photographer placed him on the front seat of the truck, put a fire hat on his head, grouped crew members on either side of him, and shot poses from a variety of different angles. A blowup of one picture was mounted and placed on the wall next to the truck.

"Where is Freckles?" Randy asked.

"He's in the backyard."

"He's not barking." Usually Freckles made an uproar every time Randy pulled into the driveway.

"He's either asleep or digging holes to China," Ruby said.

Randy lowered Marie back into the playpen. "I've got to go, Marie. Bye-bye."

She waved. "Bye-bye."

Randy smiled at Ruby. "Need to shower."

"You don't have to run to work up a sweat," Ruby said. "You can mow my yard anytime."

"Thanks." He grinned. As he walked away he realized he'd better be thinking about his own grass.

After showering he checked the clock. Time to call

Rebecca at the hospital before his lunch with Eldon. He dialed and requested her room number.

She had gone in early this morning, and he had offered to take her to the hospital. Jackie would be doing that, of course, and although they were on civil terms—amicable, as lawyers would say—he had no desire to see Jackie more than he had to. So he planned to see Rebecca this afternoon, hopefully when Jackie wasn't there.

Rebecca was having "female" trouble. Actually, the doctor called it endometriosis. Sometimes a hysterectomy was called for, but in Rebecca's case the doctor recommended a simpler operation to remove cysts.

In a moment of candor Rebecca had muttered to Randy, "If they can just stop this constipation." Randy hadn't made further inquiries about her symptoms.

He could live with losing Jackie. He didn't want to lose Rebecca, and he was relieved she would not have to undergo a hysterectomy.

Her voice came over the phone. "Hello?"

"How're you doing?"

"Randy? I'm doing fine, as fine as I could be in a place like this."

"The operation still set for tomorrow?"

"According to the doctor."

"I won't talk long now," he said, "but I'll come by to see you this afternoon."

"Good."

Randy paused. "Is Jackie there?"

"Yes. You want to speak with her?"

"No," Randy said hurriedly. "I'll see you later."

"I'll look forward to it."

Randy put the phone down gently. He thought of Jackie in the hospital room—small, petite Jackie with close-cropped black hair. But for some reason he began seeing someone taller, with long blond hair, who was looking at him eye to eye.

He met Eldon at the Wendy's on Capers Street. Eldon liked to eat there because he thought it was a class operation for fast-food service.

". . . so I think things are looking good," Eldon was saying, "at least Al thinks so." Al Perry was their lawyer. Eldon went on. "I know we can swing it. We have enough capital with the money your aunt left you and what I could borrow from Gladys's folks. And look—" Eldon brought out from his jacket a folded sheet of paper. He spread it out on the table.

"That looks like Ken," Randy said. Ken was Eldon's eight-year-old son.

"Right," Eldon said, "but it could be any kid. That's the image we want. Get the kids and the parents will come. That's Burger Boy there, and he comes to Big Burgers."

Randy nodded, examining the drawing. "Not bad."

"It's great."

"Who drew this?" Randy asked.

"A guy at the firm has a son who's studying art."

"We're going to need a lot of money."

"We'll have enough."

Randy mused. "I know we've gone over everything. When will Al finish with the proposed contract?"

"By Thursday," Eldon said, excitement choking off his voice. Randy grinned to himself. Eldon was always the can-do guy, but sometimes his dreams overran reality. He wanted out of the trucking business. As a veteran driver for Unified Van Lines he was on the road constantly. He wanted to be home more, especially with the kids at their age. He wanted a chance to make "real" money. This meant owning his own business. And owning a Big Burger franchise—sure, there was competition from Wendy's and McDonald's and Hardee's and the other national chains. But they could make Big Burger a little different. He had ideas, and he wanted to be in business with someone he could trust—his best friend Randy Stewart.

Randy looked around at the counter, the tables, the vegetable and fruit bar. Wendy's *was* a class operation. He and Eldon would have their hands full competing in the fast-food market. But the potential customers were already in place, ready to spend money, geared to go to the operation that promised them the most appealing food at the most attractive prices. And the financial return would be enormous if they could develop a following that allowed them to open other branches. They were on the ground floor. They would have the first Big Burger outlet in the city.

That afternoon, when he arrived at Rebecca's room in the hospital, he was relieved to see that Jackie wasn't there.

"Hi, Mother," he said. She held out her arms to him.

"Come here."

"Can I hug you?" he asked.

"I'm not sick," she said, embracing him.

He studied her face. "You look like you're feeling good."

"Just a little operation," she said. "Besides, I've got a special friend."

"Who's that?"

She pointed to her bedside table. The large bouquet of roses he had sent was there. But beside it was a glass figure of an angel, wings outstretched, arms beckoning. "Jackie brought me that."

He picked it up. The painting on the glass was exquisitely done—natural skin color on face and hands, colors blending softly to give the illusion of folds in the robe.

"I call him Credence."

"Credence?"

She smiled. "You can believe in him. He's my guardian angel."

He put the angel back on the table. "When can you go home?"

"Three days after the operation," she said.

"I hope things go well."

"Credence has already told me they will."

"He talked to you?"

"When you lie here and look at him, you can hear his voice. Sometimes. You can ask him a question, and then sometimes you can hear him speak to you."

"And he told you the operation will work out fine?"

"Don't you believe me?" she asked.

"If you say he spoke to you, then I believe you."

"He might speak to you, too—if you ever really need him."

"If I'm ever in the hospital, I'll try to get him to talk."

"Your angel can talk to you anytime. It isn't Credence. Your own angel who watches over you. You need to be willing to listen."

He smiled. "Mother, if he ever talks to me, I'll listen."

"So tell me," she said, relaxing on the pillow, "what's new in your life?"

He told her the deal with Big Burgers was looking better. She looked bemused.

"I hate burgers," she said.

"Luckily you're in a minority." He grinned.

"But there's something else," she said.

"What?"

"I know." She was pointing a finger. "I know there's something—" Her voice hesitated. "Or someone—have you met someone new?"

He stared at her.

"Maybe a young woman?"

"How did you know?"

She laughed. "A mother always knows." She laughed again. "Just a feeling, Randy. Or maybe it was an inner voice, maybe my angel's voice. Is there someone?"

He told her then about meeting Dani, all the circumstances.

"You mean she let you carry her to her car? She let a stranger carry her?"

He nodded. She shook her head in wonder.

"She must have been listening to a voice of her own. But that can happen, you know. You can tell things about people, when there's a special reason. When two people are supposed to meet, and—" She quit speaking, and suddenly with soft sobs she reached for her handkerchief. Randy leaned toward her.

"Mother, what's wrong?"

"Jackie's such a foolish girl," she murmured. She

looked up at Randy. "You'll find someone. Perhaps this girl is the one." She smiled. "I just want you to be happy."

He looked into her eyes. "Mother, getting to know you was worth anything that's happened between Jackie and me. I *am* happy, and you're one reason I'm happy."

She reached for his hand. He held it firmly, both of them silent in this moment of sharing a closeness not needing words.

When Randy pulled into his driveway he stopped beside the Puckett's backyard wooden fence. He noticed one wide plank was shaking at the bottom, and as he looked closer he saw a white paw emerge through a crack. Freckles the dalmatian was having a ball working on the bottom of the fence. He had loosened a plank at the bottom. A strong dog, but the Pucketts didn't want him running loose. He'd better let Ruby know about the fence so they could keep him chained until the fence was fixed.

Inside he sat next to the phone. Dani's number?—his mind was flypaper to vital information. 832-5739. He heard the ringing, and then the voice that now seemed to carry a cargo of promise.

"This is Randy," he responded.

"You remembered my number."

"The horse is out of the barn."

"What?" Her voice was perplexed.

"Pawing the ground and raring to go and not caring whether you ride bareback or not."

She laughed. "You mean you don't want to be saddled down by somebody?"

"Maybe, just maybe, the horse wouldn't mind being saddled with you."

"I see." There was a pause. "Where does the horse want to go riding?"

"To Castillo's Pub for oats and water, and Cineplex Ten afterward."

Another pause. "My next free night is Saturday."

He was relieved. That was the second night of his next two days off. "That sounds good. Seven?"

"Fine."

"I need your address."

"Sure you can remember it?" she asked.

"A horse never forgets its way home." And for some reason his heart beat faster after he said that.

"I have an upstairs apartment at 2139 Blaircroft Lane."

"Got it," he said. He waited.

"See you then," she said, softly hanging up. He slowly set the phone down. That magical voice.

He sat quietly a moment, then thought of calling Ruby about the fence. The phone rang as he was reaching.

"Hello?"

"Randy—glad you're there." His chief's voice was excited. "We've got a four-alarmer. Big warehouse on Kent Street, and they've called for our truck. They need every man they can get. Can you help us?"

"Sure."

"The truck's going out right now. Meet us at the 900 block. We have your equipment. It's going to be rough. Heavy smoke, and the whole block could be threatened."

"I'm on my way."

"Don't spare the horses," the chief said, hanging up.

My day for horses, Randy thought as he rushed to

his kitchen door, down the side steps, past the front of his car, opening his door and lunging in and banging the door shut. He fumbled with his key and poked it into the ignition. He was about to turn the key when he heard a voice.

"Stop!"

He looked to the side. No one. He craned his head toward the rear. Still no one. He started to twist the key and he heard the voice again. Clear, distinct, and strong.

"Stop!"

He looked around. No one. There was no one there. "Get out of the car," the voice said again. That didn't sound like Wiley's voice. It certainly wasn't Ruby's.

"Where are you?" Randy said. Then louder. "Where are you? What do you want?"

"I said get out of the car," came the voice. "Get out of the car now and look behind it."

Randy shook his head. "I don't know who you are or where you are, but I've got to go. We have an emergency. I'm a fireman."

The voice was louder, with a greater sense of urgency. "Get out of the car and look behind it. Do it now!"

"All right!" Randy yelled. He pushed open the door and walked to the rear of the car. And stopped, stunned. Little Marie Puckett was sitting on the ground, her back resting against his back bumper, happily playing with a shovel as she was digging dirt and scooping it into a small bucket. "Hi, Uncle Randy," she said. "Freckles ran away, but he'll be back."

Randy looked toward the fence and saw a plank

skewed to one side. Freckles had got out and Marie had followed him.

Randy hadn't heard her playing behind his car. He had been about to gun the car backward out of the driveway, until—

The voice—he had heard a voice that spoke to him as clearly as anyone ever had, a voice he had heard with his ears, a voice he had responded to with his own mouth. But there was no one here! Then he thought back to his visit with Rebecca at the hospital.

Her angel had been Credence. This voice hadn't been Credence. Rebecca had told him he had his own angel. And then he remembered his promise: "If he ever talks to me, I'll listen."

He bent down and lifted Marie into his arms. "We both have a guardian angel," he told her.

"What's a guardian angel?" she asked.

He'd have to think some more about that.

8

Delores's Angel

Remember to show hospitality. There are some who, by so doing, have entertained angels without knowing it

—HEBREWS 13:2

She was drained. No more tears. Nothing left but acceptance, and a small, hard, inner core of bitterness. The fact that her husband was dying, yes—that hurt. But many other hurts had piled up over the past years, and the weight of them all was far less heavy than this final hurt of knowing why he was dying.

As she saw him now it was hard to visualize him as he once was. Tubes were attached to both arms, oxygen was being forced into his nose, and skin lesions covered an emaciated face almost as thin as the head of a dummy skeleton in a medical anatomy class. She thought back to the time many months ago when she had learned for certain he was HIV positive.

Her doctor had tried to explain: ". . . in the absence of any other possible source of infection, we have to assume a sexual transmission. I wish he had come to me earlier."

Dr. Jerome Kinder was a close personal friend, someone who had doctored her from the time of her first marriage. They were alone in his office talking about the man she married after her first husband died.

"I'm sorry, Delores."

She thought of the way it had been the past months with Cliff. Then the face of her first husband captured her memory and she saw again the way Jeff had smiled at her on that special anniversary—their first—when he gave her a mixed bouquet of Star Gazer lilies and multicolored freesias. Dr. Kinder's words jarred her from her reverie.

"Months ago when you came to me and wanted your own HIV test, you remember what I said?—that you didn't need to worry about AIDS if you were sleeping only with your husband?"

"I remember."

"But that was the one thing worrying you."

She nodded. "I had just learned the night before that my husband was at risk."

"And you haven't been sleeping with him since that time?"

"We weren't—active—for a long time before that, either."

He looked at her reflectively. "The fact that you tested negative for HIV is, of course, a good sign, but the virus is tricky. We'll need to keep giving you periodic tests and monitor you closely."

She sat numbly. It was hard to talk. "Would it have made a difference if Cliff had come to you earlier?"

"Not after he had contracted the virus, and that

could have been years ago. We could have treated
any transient symptoms, but many times victims
think they've only got the flu or a cold. Those symptoms can manifest themselves from three to six
weeks after initial infection—malaise, diarrhea, fever,
enlarged lymph nodes, skin rash, sore throat. Then
three years or more can go by before they experience
any of the severe opportunistic infections associated
with full-blown AIDS." Dr. Kinder fiddled with a let-
ter opener on his desk. "I'm afraid your husband has
contracted one of the fastest-acting infections. The
virus made his lungs vulnerable to the bacteria
Pneumocystis carinii and *Cryptococcus neoformans*.
When the lungs are attacked no treatment can offer
much hope for delaying the inevitable."

Now she was in the hospital room again, facing reality, watching the labored breathing of a man who
seemed a stranger. But reality could not keep her
mind from reaching backward once more, and she remembered the first time she saw the house where she
lived in Pleasant Green, an area east of the city
marked by rolling hills, expansive lawns, and huge
homes with circular driveways. She remembered
pulling into the drive and coming to a stop in front of
the two-story Tudor that was exclusively listed with
her father's real estate firm.

She worked for her father, and had driven here to
become familiar with the house before trying to sell
it. But she felt instinctively that she wouldn't be selling this house; she would be buying it. She knew Jeff
would have loved it. They had been thinking about
moving and had looked at a house the weekend before the Friday he was killed driving home from
Albens, Georgia. A tractor-trailer rig jackknifed com-

ing around a sharp turn and slid on the rainy highway straight into Jeff's oncoming car.

She was still grieving after four months, but as she looked over the house memories of Jeff warmed her heart, making it beat faster until its beat was a compulsion—she had to have this house. She had loved Jeff Tolliver beyond reason. This would have been their dream house. Living here now would bring him closer to her. It was expensive, but with his life insurance she could handle the down payment and if she were careful—with her stock dividends and income from the firm—she could afford the payments. And in an emergency, her father would help her.

After graduating from Belmont University in Nashville, she had immediately gone to work for her father. She found selling real estate a natural expression of her personality—outgoing, friendly, and genuine. Clients liked her low-key approach, and their word-of-mouth to friends had built her a strong client base in only two years.

Her father was totally proud of his daughter. She was an only child, and one day would be running Knights and Associates Real Estate, Inc. But he wished she could find the right man who could enrich her life with the kind of love and companionship that marrying Joyce had given him.

The trouble was—she had poured her energies and time so relentlessly into her work that she had not had many dates, and none with anyone who interested her as a potential spouse. Until, at an engagement party for a friend from high school days, she was introduced to Jeff Tolliver.

Jeff was six feet tall, around 180, she estimated. Looked good, was well groomed, had nice manners.

But what really got to her were his eyes. They were blue, but unlike any blue she had ever seen. Light blue, but intense, with irises that seemed to be layered, so that looking into them was like going into a tunnel. They had stared at each other until she had trouble speaking. The next thing she knew was his saying something about a dance and then holding her hand and leading her to the dance floor.

Dancing with him was like moving through a cloud with wisps entering her mind, so that she had trouble hearing what he was saying. During the evening she did understand that he was thirty years old and a manufacturer's representative covering three states for six different firms. Shoe and boot factories could buy leather from him, clothing factories could get textiles, department chains could get notions of all kinds.

He was on the road a lot, but that didn't stop him from phoning her every night until she became addicted to hearing his voice. If he missed calling one night, she suffered withdrawal symptoms. When he was home she arranged her working hours so that they were together almost every moment they weren't sleeping. And one evening they were together then, too.

The next morning he cooked her breakfast before she went off to work. That evening she got home after dark. She noticed a strange station wagon parked beside Jeff's Volvo. Inside Jeff greeted her with a light kiss and then led her to the den, where she discovered a small circular table catered by a waiter from Jeffrey's, one of the city's two four-star restaurants. The table was set up in front of her stone fireplace. Flames were making wavering shadows on the white tablecloth crowned carefully with fine china and stemware. Two chairs faced each other on either side of the table. One lighted candle stood in the center and other candles were placed in strategic locations around the room. She was too stunned to speak. Jeff left the room for a moment and then returned holding out a bouquet.

She had never seen a bouquet like it. Mixed flowers—pale Star Gazer lilies surrounded by multicolored freesias of lavender, pink, and yellow. A huge bouquet of glorious beauty. She took the flowers from him and pressed them to her breast, her eyes glowing and then moistening. But now she was aware of the fragrance. Never had anything smelled as good as this special bouquet. The aroma of the Star Gazer lilies mingled with that of the freesias to make an impression of even more beauty than the sight of the flowers themselves.

During the meal, which featured filet mignon, Jeff said little. Afterward the waiter inconspicuously left the house, and Jeff held up his wineglass.

"To us," he said. They tapped glasses, and Delores thought wine had never before tasted this good. "Robert Mondavi Cabernet Sauvignon '83," he said, savoring the last swallow in his glass. Then he lowered the glass to the table and looked directly into her eyes.

"I love you," he said. "Let's get married."

She didn't have to think about it.

But two years was all they had. At twenty-seven she was alone again, and threw herself into her work harder than ever. During the next three years she stayed among the top five producers among all realtors in the city. When she was thirty she hit number two and was primed to reach the top when she first dated Cliff Meador of Bloom, Meador, Littlefield and Associates. Cliff was forty-two, specializing in corporate law. He had been divorced for five years, and his picture was often in the society pages as he appeared at various charity and civic functions, usually with a different woman on his arm.

Delores knew him casually, but had no desire beyond that since his reputation as a ladies' man made her wary. But then one night, at a charity auction for the Friends of Children's Theater, he had approached her sitting with her best friend Crystal Patton. On this occasion he was alone, and he asked if he could join her. She was polite but less than enthusiastic. Looking back, she sensed that her attitude had been a challenge to him, and his interest in her assumed spectacular dimensions during the next few weeks.

At first she refused to date him, but he wore her down with phone calls and flowers. Their first date was a surprise. They went to the Actor's Playhouse production of *You're a Good Man, Charlie Brown*. She had seen this play twice before, and thoroughly enjoyed the Peanuts characters, with their unique takeoffs on life's foibles. But she didn't expect Cliff to like it. The surprise was that he laughed and seemed to discard his usual facade of urbane sophistication. He became more human, and from that point on she began to look on him as something more than just a handsome face with roving eyes.

His pursuit was relentless. Maybe a small warning voice had always been inside her, but her loneliness responded to the continued fervency of his attention, making her deaf to any inner warning. They went on a variety of dates, and soon she marveled that she had ever had doubts about the kind of man he was. If her parents had any reservations about Cliff, they kept quiet, trusting their daughter's own instincts and remembering the depth of her happiness in her first marriage. Crystal and all her other friends wanted her to find that kind of happiness again.

When Cliff asked her to marry him she had only one condition. "I want us to live in my house," she said.

He was surprised. He had visions of building a house in the newly developed Stuart Hills subdivision. But he quickly hid his own reaction and smiled and said, "Whatever you want."

The honeymoon was a trip to Bermuda. He was properly attentive, and certainly knew the mechanics of making love. But she was a little disappointed. She talked silently to herself. What did she expect? She knew that Cliff was not Jeff. She should not expect him to be. Yet a nagging awareness of her first honeymoon, and the memory of how she had felt holding Jeff in her arms, was a constant blanket that smothered any natural exuberance in her new relationship.

Had she made a mistake?

She shouted down that small voice. She wouldn't listen to it. She had made a commitment to this new man, and she would live up to it in every way. She no longer had to be lonely. Anyway, maybe he was having doubts, too. Chances are that he was also remembering a previous marriage, at least the good times from it, and comparing her to his previous wife.

Delores knew one thing. She would not let Cliff regret anything about his new marriage. She did not expect him to forget his first wife, any more than she would forget Jeff. But their lives were planted in the present. And they would make their own memories that would enrich their future years together.

She was wrong.

After the honeymoon Cliff's attitude seemed to change—not in a radical way, but in the shadings of small everyday nuances. An increasingly proprietary tone bothered her in the way he referred to her, in the manner he decided what functions they attended or places they went. She had never thought of him as a male chauvinist, but obviously he was used to being dominant in his work and social relationships. And now he seemed to consider the marriage as his, the wife as his, and the decisions as his.

He had been different during courtship, when input was open and decisions were shared. She had expected the same qualities after marriage, the way her marriage with Jeff had been—a blend of openness and honesty and spontaneity.

She wondered why people change after the wedding ceremony. Certainly a marriage should bring changes in the pattern of daily activities, but not changes that ignored or tried to alter basic psychological needs.

Cliff's focus seemed to narrow to his work, making her feel separate. Social functions and activities were more and more posed by Cliff as responsibilities rather than options, as requirements rather than opportunities seized for the joy and pleasure of sharing them together.

But doing what was "expected" of Mrs. Cliff Meador was not Delores's ambition. She was Delores Knight, having taken back her maiden name after

Jeff's death. She had kept her name in her most recent marriage, and to her that act was more than a symbol—it represented a profound truth of her personality. Cliff had better realize it. She would not be taken for granted as an afterthought or an incidental fact of his existence.

She threw herself into her work and reached her goal of becoming the city's top producer in selling real estate. She was honored at the annual dinner of the Realtors Club as Broker of the Year. Her father and mother got their share of compliments, as well, while her husband sat beside her and basked in the reflected glory of her achievement.

Delores's peers were impressed not only by her professional ability, but by the eminently suitable marriage she had made. Cliff Meador was respected throughout the community as a senior partner in a major law firm. Add to the success each enjoyed in a career, the fact that together they simply looked good. Handsome—they made a handsome couple, a role model in these days of discordant marital relationships. Women whispered that she was so fortunate; men called him a lucky dog.

One evening when Cliff had a dinner appointment with a corporate client, something that was becoming increasingly frequent, Delores ate dinner with her parents. All of them had been strangely quiet throughout the meal.

"Del," her father said after he settled back with coffee, "your mother and I have something to talk to you about. But let me ask this first—are you all right?"

"What do you mean?"

"Do you have any kind of problem?"

"You seem unhappy, dear," her mother added.

Delores looked away. "Everything's fine."

"How are you and Cliff getting along?" her father asked.

"Why do you ask that?"

"Look, your mother and I know you pretty well. We knew when you were unhappy as a child. Remember when you got the measles and had to miss Ruth Baker's birthday party?"

She nodded. "I was ten."

"You didn't cry," he said. "You didn't get angry. You just clammed up. You wouldn't talk. Mother and I couldn't get you to say anything."

"I remember."

"You've always been that way, holding things inside, but we always knew when you were hurting. You have this wonderful outgoing personality in meeting people and working with them. That's why you're so good at selling real estate. But when it comes to something personal, something unpleasant that affects you, then you become the most private person I've ever seen."

"That's why we were so happy when you married Jeff," her mother said. "He made you open up and share your feelings. He was good for you."

Delores kept silent. Her father looked at her for a long moment.

"Is Cliff good for you?" he asked quietly.

Delores still said nothing. Finally she spoke softly. "We've had to make adjustments. Cliff is not like Jeff, but I'm also not the same woman I was with Jeff."

Her father nodded. "That's what is bothering your mother and me. You should be the same."

"What is the trouble, Delores?" her mother asked.

"Maybe I shouldn't have got married again."

Her parents watched her intently, their faces mirroring the concern they felt for their only child.

"There's not any one thing," Delores went on. "And sometimes I don't think I'm being fair to Cliff. I shouldn't compare him to Jeff. I shouldn't compare our marriage to what Jeff and I had. We were young, and Jeff died while the world was still bathed in a romantic haze. Cliff and I both have careers that demand a lot of our time, part of the price for being successful."

"Let me ask you something," her father said. "If Jeff were still alive, do you think you would have been as successful as you are now, being married to Cliff?"

She smiled at her father. "Dad, I might not have sold as much real estate, but I would have felt more successful."

Her father nodded. "I understand. You know—" he took his wife's hand, "your mother and I have always wanted you to have a rewarding career, and we wanted you to have a wonderful marriage, as we have had. We wanted you to have it all. We still do."

"Thanks, Dad."

"We can't do a lot to help your marriage, but your career—that's what your mother and I wanted to talk to you about tonight."

She waited as her father patted her mother's hand. They smiled at each other and then looked at her. "I'm thinking about retiring," he said.

"You're kidding."

"It's something your mother and I have been considering for quite a while."

Delores shook her head. "Dad, you're too young to retire."

"I could keep going," he said, "but we've got more money than we'll ever need. We'd like to travel, enjoy life while we still have our health."

"I just never thought about your being old enough to retire."

"The company's in great shape and we have someone who can run it."

Delores sat very quiet.

Her father smiled. "We have a child who's ready to take over."

"Me?" She could hardly say the word.

"We don't seem to have any other children. The company's going to be yours anyway. So have some fun with it now."

Delores's mind was moving rapidly. She was visualizing their nine agents, their support staff, their office suite on the top floor of the Baycroft Building. She was seeing herself walk into the big office with the gray leather chair behind the glass desk, and looking out the side floor-to-ceiling glass panel that looked toward a panoramic view of the skyscrapers downtown.

"Dad, I don't know—"

"Listen, you've learned every aspect of the business. You've worked hard, put in long hours, and made yourself not just our top salesperson, but the best in the whole city. No one is giving you anything. You've earned it." He smiled and glanced at his wife. "And Joyce and I have earned more time together."

Delores felt herself smiling then. Her mother leaned forward and spoke in a soft voice.

"How do you think Cliff will feel?"

Delores had no answer for that, and she really did not care.

The next morning, while riding to work, Delores got a call from Crystal on her car phone. Crystal was a buyer for the designer shop in the Crowell-Ryder Department Store.

"Glad I caught you before you got hung up with clients," Crystal said.

"I'm on my way to the office."

"Can we lunch?"

Yesterday afternoon Mr. Jacobs had called to cancel their noon appointment to see the Woolbright estate seven miles from the city. "I can make it," Delores said.

"In the Tea Room at our place? Twelve-thirty?"

"All right," Delores said. "Anything wrong?"

There was a pause. "We'll talk then. Bye."

Delores frowned, putting down the phone. She knew Crystal well enough to know something was bothering her. One thing about Crystal, she always let it all hang out.

The Tea Room was crowded, mainly with women. Some were professional career women, dressing down their normal femininity to show they could hold their own in a man's world. Other women were elderly, expensively dressed, and talking softly and rapidly as though they thought the world was listening. Two models were playing the room at the same time, going to any table where they could catch attention and hawk the materials, prices, and departments where the items could be purchased.

Crystal met her in the waiting area and led her to a table she had reserved with the hostess. A young woman in white blouse and black skirt took their orders.

"Thanks for coming," Crystal said. She waited while a model came close and made her pitch. When the model left, Crystal kept silent as though she were having second thoughts. Delores waited her out.

"Do you remember Carol Manning? She was in our aerobics class at the Y two years ago."

Delores nodded.

"I still keep up with her," Crystal said. "We, uh— ran into each other last night in the lobby of the Ultraplex 10. Ed wanted to see the Eastwood movie. Anyway, Carol asked if she could call me later. And she did, and we talked for a half hour."

"How is she?"

"She's fine. But the thing is—she works as a hostess in Creekwater's."

Delores knew of the place by reputation. A popular gay bar.

"Why would she work in a place like that?" Delores asked.

"Carol isn't gay," Crystal said. "The guy who owns it isn't, either. But Carol's boyfriend knows the owner and got her the job, and Carol says it pays more than anyplace else she could work."

Delores was curious where this conversation was headed.

"I'm not sure I should say anything," Crystal said.

"What do you mean?"

"You're my best friend, Delores. I wanted to call you and then I thought I ought to see you but now I don't know."

Delores was exasperated. "Crystal, you asked me to come here and you don't want to tell me why?"

Crystal didn't speak, then asked reluctantly, "Are you and—Cliff—getting along all right?"

"Yes."

Crystal was silent again. Delores burst out, "Go on, Crystal, tell me what you were going to say."

"Carol saw Cliff at Creekwater's."

Delores's first reaction was to tell Crystal that Cliff often took clients out for dinner or drinks. Lawyers did that. Common practice. Something that was expected. But Creekwater's—? Her mind played with that. Cliff had never mentioned going to Creekwater's. Why would his clients want to go there?

"Cliff was with three other guys," Crystal said.

"Most of Cliff's clients are men."

"Delores," Crystal said, leaning closer, "Carol saw Cliff dancing."

Delores wasn't sure how to react. "Cliff danced with a man?"

Crystal shook her head. "Carol said before they left, Cliff danced with all three men."

Delores tried to raise the water glass to her lips. She didn't make it, and her hand trembled as she lowered it back down. "I really—I really have to go." She rose then and walked hurriedly away.

Crystal called after her, then sank back in her chair, watching the trim figure in a navy power suit move past the waiting line.

Delores called the office and canceled her afternoon appointments. She went home and walked through the house, reliving their life together. What had he ever said or done to give himself away? What had she not picked up on? But don't jump to any conclusions. You know nothing—only hearsay. Her husband would laugh at hearsay. Not admissible in court. Proves nothing. Wait to hear what he says. Gay?

She had nothing against gays. She believed they had the right to choose their sexual orientation. She just had never expected to be married to one.

But he wasn't gay! He had been married before. He liked women. When he was single he had dated a lot of women. And she had made love to him. In a courtroom her personal testimony would be that he enjoyed making love to a woman.

But did he really? Their lovemaking had tapered off long ago, and now they might as well be sleeping in different beds. Which suited her. But if he liked women and men—

Bisexual?

She sat in the big lounge chair by the front window in the living room. Sunlight poured past draperies and pressed her head and shoulders with warmth. She watched the shadows on the rug move and dim with time until, in the twilight, furniture stood as mute ghosts mourning the dying sun. Eventually she heard a car approaching and a door slam. The door opened and Cliff switched on the overhead light.

"Delores?" he said, blinking as he focused on her.

"Let's talk."

He moved close to her. "What's wrong?"

"Sit down," she said. He sat on the nearby couch.

"Why did you marry me?" she asked.

"What are you talking about?"

"Are you gay?"

He stared at her, stunned, and then she knew.

"No lies. No excuses. I want the truth, all of it."

"I don't know what you're talking about."

"You were *seen!*" she exclaimed. "Now talk to me!"

He stood up then. He moved around the room, looking at a picture, a chair, a vase, vacantly staring as though hearing voices where each was trying to be heard above all the others. Finally, he turned to her.

"Creekwater's?"

"Yes."

"I knew we shouldn't have gone there. We had been drinking, and I thought there would be little chance you could hear anything. Or anyone else who knew me."

He sat down again, and the words began to flood out. He had had his first gay encounter in college. But he also liked women. And he had ambition, which meant a wife, a home, and hopefully children to complete the image as he moved upward in his career. His first marriage hadn't worked out because, even then, he had been unable to sustain his passion for his wife. She had strong biological needs, and she moved on. But he still wanted a home and a wife who could entertain in that home. And he had fallen in love with her.

Yes, he truly loved her. But she could not satisfy him fully. No woman could. Periodically his inner hunger drove him to seek men.

"How many?" she asked.

"What do you mean?"

"How many men have there been?"

He hesitated. "A few."

"A few in our marriage, or do you mean a few in both marriages, or just a few in all the time since college?"

"This is crazy—"

"Tell me!" she shouted.

He wouldn't speak.

"While we've been married, have there been a number of men who slept with you?"

"You've got to understand, Delores," he said, "I—I have my own needs."

She jumped up. "That's it! I want you out of here."

"No, Delores—" He caught at her arm.

"Now!" she yelled, twisting away.

"I'll leave. But don't cause a scandal. It wouldn't be any better for you than for me."

She thought of her parents then. She thought of her business, of the new job waiting for her. And she thought of Jeff. *Jeff, why did you have to die?*

In calmer voices, then, she and Cliff worked out an arrangement. They would still live in this house together, but in different bedrooms. They would make plans to get a divorce, but everything would proceed in an amicable and civil manner. Then Delores thought of something else.

"What about AIDS?" she asked.

"There's no danger."

"Of course there's danger."

"I've always been careful," he said.

"Great. You know how many people are HIV positive? A newspaper article said more than two million."

"But we don't need to worry."

"I need to worry," she said. "I'm going to see Dr. Kinder tomorrow and get tested."

"What are you going to tell him?"

"I'm going to tell him I want to be tested."

"He'll ask why."

"Don't worry. I won't tell him that I have a husband who's been sleeping around with gay men."

"I haven't been sleeping around."

"And if you're smart, you'll get tested right away."

But he didn't get tested right away. Not until the persistent cough. Not until his weight began to fall off. By that time divorce proceedings were well under way, but after diagnosis of full-blown AIDS she had halted the proceedings. Now in the hospital room she was glad she was still Cliff's wife. She had been able to comfort him in his pain, and perhaps give him added courage to face what was coming.

A widow again. Soon she would have the memory of two dead husbands. Would Jeff meet Cliff? Would he be able to welcome Cliff to another realm, where Cliff once more could breathe easy and have the strength to sit up and walk and talk? Would they talk about her? What would they say about the woman— still young—who stayed behind on the earth? Would they want her to meet someone new and fall in love, to get married again?

Oh, Jeff, Jeff—you were my one true love. Forever young in my heart, forever the one who held me in the first bloom of love, the one who painted the future as a rainbow of beauty, the one who on our first anniversary gave me a bouquet that smelled sweeter than the breath of angels.

She sat in the chair, slumped back with her head resting on a pillow, her eyes closed, when she heard the voice.

"Delores?"

She opened her eyes, dazed at first. Someone had called her. Then she heard it again.

"I'm here, Delores."

She turned to the sound of the voice. Someone was standing there, one arm held behind him.

"Jeff—?" she muttered, not believing what she saw. It couldn't be Jeff. Jeff was dead.

"It's me," he said. She tried to stand up and almost fell, her knees buckling. He moved to her and put his free arm around her for support.

"How could—?" She touched his arm. She pressed against his chest. Then she drew back. "No. I'm dreaming."

"Is this a dream?" he asked, and from behind him brought a bouquet. Star Gazer lilies mixed with freesias—pink, lavender, and yellow. Their bouquet, their special bouquet! She buried her face in the flowers. The aroma, the sweet, beautiful aroma, unlike any other flowers on earth. Unique fragrance, like their love had been. This *was* Jeff! Jeff had come back to her! She hugged him, crushing the flowers between them. She felt his hand stroking her hair and heard the same voice that had whispered to her as they lay holding each other in bed.

"Everything will be all right, Delores. You'll be all right. Cliff will be all right."

She started crying then. It felt so good to cry, to hold Jeff in her arms. Finally her crying stopped, and she was content just to stand close to him. She panicked when she felt him pulling away.

"Where are you going?"

"I've got to go back."

"You can't!" she said. "Not again. You can't leave me again!"

He smiled at her. "I'll never leave you. You'll always find me in your heart." He started to back away.

"No. Jeff, come back, please—"

He opened the door, still looking at her, his blue eyes more penetrating than ever. He held up the flowers and gave a little wave, and with one final smile he closed the door behind him.

Delores wanted to cry again, but she was dry inside. No more tears. And that hadn't been Jeff. Jeff was dead. But she saw someone. An angel? Could an angel look like Jeff? Who knew what an angel looked like. Maybe an angel could look like anyone.

She sat back down, slumping against the chair cushion and positioning the pillow behind her head. She closed her eyes, but she wasn't able to rest long. A hand was shaking her shoulder. She looked up and saw a nurse.

"I'm sorry. I'm afraid your husband is gone."

She looked at the bed. Another nurse and a doctor were removing the various tubes and needles. Delores felt relief, and then a sharp disappointment. It had been a dream, only a dream. She didn't see Jeff. She didn't see an angel. She had been asleep and only dreaming.

"Something's very strange," the nurse said.

"What?"

"You know we weren't allowed to have flowers in this room, with your husband's breathing difficulty. But I smell flowers." The nurse turned to the other nurse. "Do you smell flowers?"

The other nurse breathed deeply. "Yes, but I can't make out what they are."

"Not roses," the first nurse said.

"I know what they are." Delores was smiling. "Star Gazer lilies and freesias."

9

Dennis's Angel

God employs them as messengers to manifest himself to men

—Calvin

Dennis Roper didn't know much about soccer, but he knew his son's team was getting beaten badly. An inexperienced new coach and many inexperienced new players didn't make for a winning combination. When Alan started playing in the YMCA youth league three years ago he had been assigned right fullback, mainly protecting his own goal. But he was aggressive and was soon made right halfback. Then this year the coach made him center forward, with major responsibility for scoring.

The trouble was the team had trouble moving the ball close enough to the opponent's goal for a scoring attempt. Alan was always willing to rush forward and keep his leg kicking amid other pumping legs and accept the bruising contact sometimes necessary for gaining control of the ball. But any continuing control of the ball always lasted about as long as a cat's restive state in a dog pound.

"They'll learn," Coach Murphy told Dennis after the first game of the season. Three games later they still had a lot to learn. So Dennis watched and kept his face impassive when nearby fathers and mothers yelled with glee after another goal was scored against Alan's team.

The score was 7–0 in the waning minutes. Dennis was resigned to the loss, but it galled him to see the goose egg. Skunked again—the second week in a row his son's team had not scored any points. A loss is a loss, right? Wrong.

All his life Dennis had heard that losing by one point is just as bad as losing by ten points. Some losing players even said they felt *worse* when they lost by only one point.

Dennis didn't believe it. He had played basketball in high school, and he knew what winning and losing felt like. The winners felt great regardless of the point difference. They felt as good winning by twenty points as winning by one. But on the losing side—it definitely felt worse to lose by a lot than by a little.

And in sports like tennis, baseball, or soccer a goose egg was the king of hurt. To play your heart out and not score any points—no matter what sport— was the loss with the biggest memory.

Action on the field suddenly quickened Dennis's pulse rate. Three forwards on the opposing team were threatening, dribbling and kicking the ball adroitly to each other in avoiding the defensive halfbacks and fullbacks while moving down the field. One forward was poised to attempt the kick when he stumbled, twisting his ankle. A defending fullback captured the ball and kicked it as hard as he could in the opposite direction. The ball took flight over colliding bodies and Alan captured it in midfield. He maintained control, dribbling and moving rapidly as an opposing halfback rushed toward him. He kicked the ball to his left forward across the field, who kept it moving downfield. The opposing right fullback was rushing toward him, and he kicked it back to Alan who was racing up the middle of the field, moving straight toward the goal. The defending left fullback moved to block him and he slanted to the right. This was the closest Alan's team had been to the opponent's goal all afternoon.

The goalie was moving back and forth in front of the goal, trying to anticipate the direction of Alan's kick. Alan shifted his shoulders to the left, his leg poised to kick. The goalie moved to his right, and Alan kicked just as the fullback crashed into him. The ball sailed shoulder-high to the goalie's left. He made a desperate leap to deflect it.

Too late. The ball plunged into the net, and Alan was leaping up and down like he had won the Super Bowl. His teammates came running to him. The coach was yelling. And Dennis was pacing back and forth, nodding and smiling and feeling like he had just landed a contract for carpeting the new Sheraton Hotel scheduled to be built downtown.

On their way home Alan spent a lot of time griping about the game, with Dennis trying to console him and talking about the improvement he could see in the team's play.

"What we need is a little divine help—like Leslie's angel," Alan said, his voice sarcastic.

Dennis smiled. "Maybe he helped you on that kick."

"Man, that felt good, you know? I knew I could get it in."

"So you think the angel helped you?"

"Dad." Alan looked exasperated. "If we really had an angel, we would be winning some games." He was silent a moment. "But I think you ought to talk to Leslie."

"She's OK."

"But it isn't normal."

"You had an invisible friend when you were a child."

"Not at her age. And my friend wasn't an angel."

Dennis glanced at Alan. "Your grandmother believes in angels at eighty-six."

"That's different."

"You're used to hearing her talk about angels. That's probably where Leslie got the idea for her own angel."

"But Grandma doesn't go around acting like an angel's always at her side. I mean, Leslie says an angel moves her hands on the keys."

Leslie was taking piano lessons, and after a difficult practice would sometimes say an angel guided her hands to play the right notes.

"I don't see where that's a problem," Dennis said. "If she feels an angel helps her, it may give her more confidence."

"But she talks about it to my friends. They think she's weird."

Dennis nodded. "I see. You're thinking about a friend named Ruby?"

"Not just Ruby."

"But Ruby's the main one, right?" Ruby Townsend lived only two blocks away, someone Alan had known from early childhood. They had attended the same schools, and now in the eighth grade had discovered a mysterious attraction that made them want to study together and go places together and simply be together.

"If Leslie just wouldn't mention her angel," Alan said. "Lauren doesn't talk about angels."

Dennis smiled at that thought. Lauren didn't talk much about anything. Leslie and Lauren were twins, but they couldn't be more unlike. They didn't dress alike or look alike. Fraternal twins, as distinct as strangers.

Leslie was petite, with dark skin, brown eyes, and black hair—taking after her mother. Lauren was taller, lighter skinned with blond hair and blue eyes, showing genetic kinship to her father. But personality was the most striking contrast. Leslie was always talking, an energetic extrovert who had made the phone a grafted appendage to her ear. Lauren was quiet and sky, introverted to the point where communication often depended on a stare and instinct.

"Look," Dennis said, "I'm sorry if Leslie embarrasses you in front of your friends. But she says what she feels. We have to accept her as she is."

"She's old enough to stop talking about imaginary friends. She knows Santa Claus isn't real. So why carry on about an angel?"

Dennis shook his head. "Alan, if Leslie thinks she has a guardian angel, fine."

"Watch it!" Alan yelled. A pickup truck appeared coming over the rise of the hill and was partially on their side of the line. Dennis swerved to the right as brakes squealed before the truck lurched to the other side of the road.

"That guy was crazy!" Alan said. Dennis slowed down. The road was full of hills and turns as it passed by cattle farms on its way to the outlying county park where the soccer field was located.

Dennis looked at Alan and grinned. "Maybe an angel kept us from hitting that truck. What do you think?"

"I'd have to *see* an angel before I'd believe it."

Dennis slowed down more when he saw the cow. Then very slow. The cow was walking aimlessly next to the road.

"Someone's going to hit one of Sligar's cows if he doesn't keep them away from the road," Dennis said.

"Seems like he's always working on his fence," Alan said.

"He needs to hire someone who can do it right, and fix his gate, too."

When the car got past the cow, Dennis sped up.

Not much was said the rest of the way home. Dennis began thinking about a phone call he had to make. When they got to Beechwood Avenue Alan grew restive.

"Dad," he said, "can you let me out at Ruby's house?"

"Sure."

"I want to tell her about my goal."

Dennis stopped the car before a large two-story brick home with a large screened-in porch on one end. The house looked expensive, but all the houses in the Palmdale area were upscale, and especially here on Beechwood. Alan waved and went running toward the house.

Two blocks farther Dennis pulled into the drive-way of a rambling ranch-style home of holiday stone. He had a huge backyard with a high wooden fence that gave privacy for a tennis court and outdoor bar-becue parties.

Inside the house he heard the familiar broken notes of Leslie's piano practice.

"Hi, Punkin," he said. Leslie's face lighted up.

"Daddy—listen!" She played a simple melody line. "I wrote that," she said. "How do you like it?"

"I like it," he said, smiling. "Where's your mother?"

"She went to Darwinkle's with Mrs. Barrow." Gracie Barrow was Lucille's best friend. "They're looking at French antiques," she added.

Antiques were Gracie's major passion, and Lucille enjoyed going with Gracie on her frequent excursions to search for the ultimate elusive hidden treasure.

"Where's Lauren?"

"Reading, I guess, in the den."

Dennis moved to the den, finding his quiet daugh-ter curled up on the couch. He appreciated the fact that Lauren largely ignored TV. The other two chil-dren found the tube endlessly fascinating, but Lauren had always acted like it was a second-class citizen.

"Hi, Dad," she said when he poked his head in.

"What are you reading?"

"I got it from the library," she said. *The True Be-liever.*

He was surprised. *The True Believer* by Eric Hoffer, the book Eisenhower had made famous by recommending it to his cabinet members. How many ten-year-olds read that book?

"How do you like it?" he asked.

"I have to look up a lot of the words in the dictionary," she said, "but his ideas are simple and logical. And I like the way he writes in short blocks. He numbers them and if you don't understand something, you can stop and think about it."

He nodded. He needed to read that book again.

In his study he picked up the phone and hesitated. He had to make this call, but he dreaded it. Max Harper was an old friend of his, and he trusted his accounting firm of Harper and Puryear always to act in the best interests of the Roper-York Tile and Carpet Supply Company.

He listened to the phone ringing. No answer. He was about to hang up when he heard the familiar scratchy voice. "Hello?"

"Hey, Max—it's Dennis."

"We need to talk."

"I know we do, and I hope what you say makes sense." There was a silence.

"We need to talk in person," Max said.

Dennis felt something cold shift in his stomach. "All I wanted was for you to explain that note from Carruthers."

"It would be better if I see you."

"All right. When do you want to meet?"

"Now? Can you come to my office?"

"I'll be there."

"I'll tell the guard to expect you." Max hung up. Dennis let the phone down gently, leaning back in his chair. He thought back on the beginning of the company. He and Cecil York made an ideal team—Cecil the Mr. Inside, Dennis Mr. Outside. Cecil took care of the books, handled the financial details of the nitty-gritty daily operation while Dennis concentrated on sales and customer relations.

The Roper-York Tile and Carpet Supply Company retailed through their showrooms on Danner Street and seven other sites, including three other cities. They also bid on construction jobs in a five-state area, furnishing crews that would lay carpet and tiles in office towers and hotels of all sizes. The point where Dennis tried to differentiate his company from competitors was the follow-up service and support. He took pride in checking behind his workers, and maintaining periodic contact with clients to ensure their continuing satisfaction. He had computerized all his clients for dated contracts which were personal and informal, and which, hopefully, were pointed toward future business.

The company had grown in its sixteen years, becoming even more aggressive in the past year, when they had opened up three new showrooms. They also had moved to new local headquarters and added personnel.

Cecil had assured him the business was on a solid foundation for all this expansion, and he was satisfied with his own viewing of the projections. But then he got a note from Carruthers, a personal friend at the bank, that their cash reserve was dangerously low to meet their debt obligations. An inquiry to his partner brought a pat on the back that the situation was only temporary, and he should not worry. That's when he had asked Max to investigate quietly and give him a personal report.

He stood up and left his study, meeting his wife coming in.

"How was the game?" she asked.

"Lost, but Alan scored a point."

"Good."

"I dropped him off at Ruby's house."

"Where are you going?"

"I've got to go see Max Harper. I'll be back before dinner."

"You have to work?"

"Just a brief conference." He kissed her. "See you soon."

"How do you like this?" she asked, holding up a figurine of a young woman. "A Louis XIV lady-in-waiting. Not a real antique—a replica, but beautiful, isn't it?"

He nodded. He was glad he wasn't paying for a real antique.

Max Harper seemed nervous, which made Dennis nervous. "Sit down, Dennis. Anything to drink?"

Dennis shook his head. Max went to his liquor cabinet and poured some Scotch. One swallow and then he smiled at Dennis.

"You need that for what you're going to tell me?" Dennis asked.

Max moved to his window and looked out. Then he turned slowly to face Dennis and sat in his chair behind the desk. He leaned forward and played with some papers in front of him.

"First, you are in a tight situation, but I think you'll be all right."

"Explain."

"You can meet your current debt obligations, but your cash flow is not sufficient to meet both your operating expenses and future debt retirement. You may need to cut back."

"We've just expanded! What kind of double-talk is this? I've looked at the projections."

"You've expanded too fast, Dennis."

"Wait a minute. You're my accountant, right? You've been aware of everything we've done. Why haven't you said anything?"

"I warned Cecil."

"Why didn't you talk to me?"

"He asked me not to. He said everything would work out and it would be better not to bother you."

Dennis tried to get control, and spoke in a calm voice. "I thought we were friends."

"We are, Dennis. Believe me. But Cecil is your partner, and I thought he would confer with you. Then when you went ahead with the expansion, I thought you were aware of everything."

"But the projections looked good."

"They were—optimistic."

Max took a pencil out of the drawer and began aimlessly to draw figures on the paper in front of him. "You borrowed heavily based on those projections and the contracts you had already landed for the next eighteen months."

"And the risk was within acceptable boundaries."

"How many of those contracts have you lost?"

"Several—but they'll come back."

"The fact is, they paid you a penalty to get out of those contracts."

"No one knew the economy would go south."

"You're right, Dennis," Max said. "No one knew. And unless you cut expenses, you're going to eat into savings and capital needs just to stay afloat."

"Unbelievable."

"I'm really sorry."

"How could I be so dense?"

Max kept silent.

"Cecil and I are going to have to learn to talk a little more," Dennis said drily. "Partners should talk to each other, don't you think?"

"I thought you knew the situation and I was surprised when you asked me to do a little investigating."

Dennis smiled thinly. "So, actually, you didn't have to do any investigating."

"I did make a few contacts—" Max hesitated. "There may be another problem." He breathed deeply and looked around as though he were trying to see a landscape he could visit outside this room.

"The contract you're working on now—the Westgate Professional Building. I've got a friend who works in their business office, and he told me of a rumor."

"What rumor?"

"You won the contract with low bid?"

"Right."

"He says you may have been tipped."

Dennis sat stunned.

"I made that bid. We weren't tipped."

"Didn't Cecil talk you down? Didn't he convince you that you could cut some more?"

"Yes, but we always confer on bids. He stays closer to costs and sources."

"You were the last to bid and the rumor is that you knew what you had to beat."

"That's not true. Why would anyone at Westgate let us know the low bid?"

Max stared at him. Finally Dennis caught on. "Payoffs?"

Max nodded. "The rumor is that someone at

Westgate got money for passing along information about the bids."

"Cecil wouldn't do anything like that."

Max was silent. Then finally he spoke in a soft voice. "I don't have any real facts, just a feeling I've had for several years. Cecil does all your purchasing, doesn't he?"

"Yes."

"I've always had the impression that he lives higher on the ladder than you."

"His wife has money, but what difference does that make?"

"Cecil is the one who deals directly with your sources?"

"Yes."

"Payoffs can work on many levels. That's all I'll say."

Dennis didn't want Max to say any more. All he wanted was to get out of that office and go home where he could deal with simple problems, such as a ten-year-old girl who played the piano with an angel.

The moment he got in the front door Lauren approached him holding *The True Believer.* "Daddy, Hoffer says we're unhappier when we have a lot and want something more, than we are if we have nothing and then want something. But people with nothing would be the unhappiest, wouldn't they?"

"Let me see."

She handed him the book. "Number 23," she said.

He studied the words, then looked at her. "No—he's saying that rich people who are trying to get richer are actually more frustrated than poor people who don't have nearly as much."

"That doesn't seem right. Poor people would be the unhappiest."

He smiled. "Hoffer could be wrong. But he makes you think."

The next voice he heard was Leslie's. "Daddy, listen to this." She played him a tune.

"Sounds good," he said.

"My angel gave me that song."

He smiled and headed for the kitchen. His wife was working on a salad. "Dinner's almost ready."

He kissed her on the cheek. "Is Alan back?"

She nodded. "In his room."

"I need to phone Cecil and see if I can meet with him tonight."

"Anything wrong?"

"I just need to ask him about something."

In his study he stared at the phone. The second time today he would make a phone call he didn't want to make. He picked up the phone. After dialing he waited. "Cecil?"

"Right," came the familiar voice. "Dennis, is that you? How'd the game go?"

"We're improving."

"It's been hectic here all day, but the driveway is finished." Cecil was resurfacing with granite-mix concrete.

"Good," Dennis said. "Cecil, we need to talk."

"Sure."

"Tonight?"

Cecil's voice was cautious. "Anything the matter?"

"Something I need to ask you about."

"I told you not to worry about the debt retirement schedule."

"Something else, Cecil. Let's meet where we can be alone."

"How about coming over here? Gladys will be playing bridge at Elaine Stockton's house."

"Eight o'clock all right?"

"Fine. See you then."

Dennis was always impressed when he came to Cecil's home. He was impressed by the neighborhood with its large tree-sheltered lots and high stone fences and long driveways. Cecil did live higher on the ladder, but he had always alluded to his wife's money as the reason why he could live in Stanton Hills. Could there be another reason?

Cecil answered the door, welcoming him with an expansive smile, but his eyes carried worry lines. Or was this Dennis's imagination? Cecil took him to the library and offered him a glass of wine. He opened a bottle.

"Joseph Phelps 1989 Cabernet Sauvignon Insignia," he said, pouring two glasses. "Phelps is one of my favorite California vineyards." He took a sip. "A glass of wine each day is good for the heart, you know."

Dennis took a sip. "Very nice."

Cecil sat in a large black leather lounge chair. "Now what did you want to talk about?"

"I'm still troubled about our financial position."

"I told you that was temporary. We're in good shape."

"Max is concerned, too."

"When did you talk to him?"

"This afternoon."

Cecil took another drink, examining his glass. "Max doesn't always give good advice."

"I had asked him to do a little investigating."

"Oh?"

"He heard a rumor."

Cecil smiled. "Rumors are everywhere."

"He heard that we knew the low bid on the Westgate job."

Cecil looked at his glass again, not speaking. Then he put the glass down and stood up, going over to a bookcase and looking at titles. Then he turned back to Dennis.

"We did know."

"We broke the law?"

Cecil moved back to his chair and sat. "What I did is done all the time. Sometimes you have to help things along a little. We had lost four bids in a row."

"You paid someone for information?"

"Of course."

"And you never told me?"

"Look, we've met a lot of obstacles and overcome them. But I've always known you were Mr. Straight Arrow. That makes it nice to be partners with you, but it doesn't always make it easy to land contracts. People who pass out jobs want something laid in their palms."

Dennis stood. "We don't do business that way. *I* don't do business that way. We're through."

"What do you mean?"

"Call your lawyer. My lawyer will be talking to him about the quickest way to dissolve our partnership."

"I'll buy you out."

Dennis smiled. "You mean you have enough money? Oh, I forgot—you have your wife's money."

"You're a fool, Dennis."

"You won't be buying my name in the deal. That isn't for sale." Dennis left as Cecil stared after him. He took a final swallow from the glass. Empty. He put the glass down on the table and decided not to pour any more wine. It didn't taste good any more.

A week later, when Dennis was driving Alan to his next soccer game, he reflected on how much had changed in that short time. Lawyers were doing their work. Cecil was buying him out. And he was already making plans to start a new business. The contract would prevent him from competing with Cecil, but Dennis had long been interested in starting a family-food restaurant. His kids were at the right age for shoveling in burgers and fries and shakes, and he had his own ideas on how to appeal to kids their age while offering a more healthful menu that would attract their parents.

The weather was threatening. As Dennis drove up a hill and moved around a curve a gust of wind splashed a few drops of rain on the windshield.

"The game may be called off," Dennis said.

Alan responded, "It may not be raining on the field."

The sprinkles came faster now, and Dennis switched on his wipers. "Or we may need an ark to get back home," he said.

"Go on out there," Alan said.

Dennis kept driving.

Alan looked at his watch. "We're late."

Dennis sped up. The rain came down harder, and was continuous. They went up another hill, then down and around another curve. Then up another hill when Alan suddenly jabbed Dennis's arm.

"Look, over there! That guy is waving his arms."

Dennis glanced at the right side of the road. Standing in tall weeds was an elderly man wearing a floppy black hat. He looked like a fugitive from the Ozarks.

"What does he want?" Dennis asked.

"I don't know. It looks like he wants us to slow down."

Dennis let up on the accelerator. "Does he need help?"

"I don't think so. He's nodding and making some motion with his hands."

By this time Dennis had slowed way down. He was past the man and near the top of the hill. "I can't stop here and go back. We'll turn around over the hill."

When they got to top of the hill Dennis suddenly slammed on his brakes. The car skidded ahead ten feet, coming to a stop five feet from a cow which was standing crossways in his lane.

"That old man was warning us about the cow," Dennis said.

Alan nodded. "We would have hit it for sure."

"If we had, we would have totaled the car, the cow, and maybe us." He hurriedly turned the car around and went back over the hill. "Do you see him?" Dennis asked.

"No, but he was standing right over there."

Dennis pulled the car off the side of the road. "He's got to be around."

The rain had almost stopped now, but the grass and weeds were wet. Dennis and Alan moved to where they thought the man had been standing. They looked in all directions. No trees, no rocks, nothing to hide behind. He couldn't have just disappeared.

"Where could he be?" Alan asked. "You saw him, didn't you, Dad?"

"Yes. He was there."

They moved in bigger circles. "OK," Dennis said, "he had to leave tracks. Look at the tracks we're making." Their feet left deep impressions in the wet weeds. But they found no impressions of any kind except their own.

"Let's go," Dennis said.

In the car moving toward the park they were both quiet. Finally Alan spoke. "Dad, we could have been hurt bad."

Dennis nodded. Alan went on. "Do you think— that could have been an angel?"

"We both saw him, right?"

"Yes," Alan said.

"And we saw no signs of footprints or tracks in the grass."

"There weren't any."

"I'd say that was impossible, wouldn't you?"

They were silent again for a long while. "Dad, why would an angel look like that?"

"He got our attention, didn't he?"

After another moment. "Do you think anyone will believe us?"

Dennis grinned. "Leslie might."

10

Victor's Angel

For he has charged his angels to guard you
wherever you go, to lift you on their hands for
fear you should strike your foot against a stone
—PSALMS 91:11–12

His fingers fumbled with his tie. This is ridiculous. Why was he going? He hadn't bothered to go to any of his *own* high school reunions, so why this one? He wouldn't know anyone. He wasn't a good dancer. He was awkward meeting new people. He wasn't a good conversationalist.

Hundred-percent, he thought, staring at himself in the mirror—hundred-percent loser.

Only one reason he was going. Marion had asked him to go. The mysteries of women. She was four years younger than he, and even more beautiful than Paula, the wife—now dead—whom he had adored. So why had Marion Chester looked him straight in the eyes and asked, "Victor Richie, will you go with me to my fifteen-year high school reunion?"

She didn't look like she had graduated that long

ago. She certainly didn't look thirty-four, while he
looked every minute of his thirty-eight years.

He had seen her first at church, when Paula was
still alive. During the nine years he and Paula had
been married they never missed Sunday School and
church unless they were out of town. The Elm Street
Baptist Church only had 525 members, so everyone
knew everybody else.

Marion's parents were pillars in the church, and
when Marion got married, the whole church was invited, including him and Paula. He vividly remembered how beautiful Marion looked as she moved
down the aisle in a floor-length white gown. A lot of
folks thought she looked too young to get married—
she was only eighteen—but everyone loved the Chesters and their daughter and hoped the marriage would
work out.

It didn't.

Her husband turned out to be a wife beater. She
stayed with him four years before she finally sought
help. His family was wealthy, and his father, president of South States Capital Management, Ltd., was
so mortified he made sure Marion got a huge settlement in the divorce as well as the house and ongoing
financial support for their one child—a son.

Everyone thought Marion would get married again.
She was still very young and had a lot of emotional
support from her friends. But she took back her
maiden name, left home, and went to Nashville,
where she found a good day-care center for the child
and took a business degree at Belmont University.
Then she came back home and started a florist business. People figured her former father-in-law helped
her get started. In any case, during the next six years

her business had grown and now was one of the city's three largest.

Victor and Paula Richie's favorite place to sit in church was two rows behind the Chesters, more toward the center. Church members' talk about Marion reflected a curiosity and even concern that it was too bad she had never found another man. She obviously dated. Sometimes a new face would show up with her in church.

But nothing happened.

Paula never liked any gossip about Marion. "She was abused by a man," she said. "That can take a long time to get over. Anyway, her hands are full running a business and raising a child."

Victor and Paula had tried to have children, without success. The doctor could never pinpoint why. Victor's sperm count was high enough. Paula thought it had to be her fault. And then when she developed her heart condition, she was certain of it. The doctor said there was no connection, but she didn't believe him.

She had always tended to feel fatigue, but she thought this was just a normal condition of her peculiar metabolism. Some people simply had a below average energy level. But she began on some occasions to to be aware of her heart, feeling—and sometimes even thinking she could hear—her heart beat. This did not alarm her until the first heart palpitations and chest pains three years ago.

Victor had rushed her to a heart specialist. A chest X-ray showed her heart was enlarged. The diagnosis was cardiomyopathy, probably of the hypertrophic type. Usually this disorder was inherited, but actually the causes were unknown. The doctor put her on an antiarrhythmic drug and had her come in for regular monitoring.

When she developed edema and had increasing difficulty in breathing, the doctor talked to Victor alone. He quietly explained there was no treatment other than the drug already given, and the diuretic drug he was about to prescribe. But with her condition the heart muscle function steadily deteriorates, and the speed of that process varies with the patient. Victor had best be prepared for whatever happened.

What happened was that her condition worsened until she had to go to the hospital. All the church family rallied behind them, and Marion was one of those who came to visit Paula in the hospital.

Then one night Paula took Victor's hand and held it and in a weak voice said she was soon going to leave him. He wanted to argue, but something in her face kept him silent. "Victor, we've had some good times."

He nodded.

"I don't think any other man could have made me so happy. I just wish—I could have left you with a child."

"No, Paula, you were always enough."

She smiled. "Your hands built our house. But your heart gave me a home."

He could only look at her, trying to keep tears from showing. Yes, he would have liked to have a child, a little girl, one that would always remind him of her mother. This woman who had bowled with him, who was a ferocious competitor in bridge, who volunteered at the Red Cross Center every Tuesday, who packed lunch for him on the days when his jobs made it inconvenient to find an eating place, who lis-

tened and consoled him when he had trouble with his
brother, who sat beside him every Sunday at church—
this woman had been his life.

"Victor, I want to tell you something. I know I'm
leaving soon because of my dream. I saw this
figure—it's funny—I don't know if it was a man or
woman. A glowing mist of light and through it I
could see this figure, and the voice, the voice I
heard—" she stopped, as though fighting to breathe,
then relaxed, "—an angel—told me not to worry. I
would soon be coming to my new home, but—Victor,
the angel told me something else."

Victor waited, still holding her hand. He had always been aware of her belief in angels. She even
carried a little golden replica of an angel figure in her
purse at all times. As for himself, he recognized their
role in the Bible, but he had never viewed angels as
being practical for today's world.

"Victor, the angel said he would watch over you
after I'm gone." She looked at him as though wanting
a reaction, but all he could do was hold her hand to
his face and kiss it. Now he couldn't keep the tears
from showing.

"Victor, one other thing. I want you to find someone else."

"Please—" He didn't want to hear this.

"I know what you're feeling. But listen, you are a
good man, Victor. Too good not to make some other
woman happy, and have her make you happy. Besides," she said smiling, "you are still young. You
can have children."

"I want only you," he said, placing his head on her
chest. She smoothed his hair.

"Dear, dear Victor. You will be all right. You will

remember what I said. The angel will watch over you. He promised . . ." Her voice faded, and Victor quickly lifted his head. He looked at her, seeing her closed eyes, seeing her chest move in slow and now more peaceful breathing, and he cried.

That night she died.

Victor finished with the tie. That would have to do. Along with everything else about him, he had done all he could. His best suit—dark blue—new shirt, polished shoes, fresh shave, and shampoo. If he just had a new body. Of course, he thought, eyeing himself in the mirror, some things about this body weren't bad. His muscle tone was hard—from both the physical labor of his construction business and the weight training regimen he had followed since college days. His heart was in good shape from his jogging. But his face—not exactly alluring to Hollywood talent agents. Beauty and the beast—that's what Marion's high school friends probably would say.

Still—she had asked him to take her. So why debunk someone who at least holds some kind of appeal to a woman like Marion? Victor filled his pockets with comb, handkerchief, coins, wallet, and—

He picked up the key ring last. A little metal chain circled the ring of keys, and on the chain hung the little golden angel his wife had carried. He had taken the figure to a jeweler who had affixed a small clasp at the top, and through it inserted a thin golden chain that could then be attached to the key ring. The angel was always with him, carried not for protection, but for the memory of the love he had shared with his wife.

A tap on his door, and then it opened with a head peeking through.

"Ready yet?"

"Yes."

"You don't want to be late."

"You sound like Paula." Not exactly true. His brother Mike did not sound like Paula, but Paula had a fetish about being on time. "You remember what I said, Mike?"

"Sure."

"About tonight. I want to talk to you when I get back."

"I'll be here."

"No late-night stuff."

"I said I'd be here."

Downstairs Victor picked up a couple of albums he had recently bought that contained oldies from the seventies. He had checked with a music store for titles, and found out that 1977 produced varied hits like "Da Doo Ron Ron" and "You Light Up My Life." Talk about contrast.

Victor's chief indulgence was his car. He had bought a four-year-old Porche 910 from someone whose house he remodeled, and he kept it purring like a cat on catnip. Dark green, with a pickup rate that could make his belly button shake hands with his backbone. Not that he ever opened it up. He just liked knowing it had the potential.

Victor knew where Marion's house was. He had been working on it for more than three weeks. She wanted extensive remodeling on the kitchen and den areas, new carpet in the dining and living areas, new bath fixtures, tearing down the wall between two bedrooms on the second floor to create a large studio room with skylights, and a new roof. His construction company was prepared for all these jobs, and more. Actually, he often took assignments where he was chief contractor, building homes from the ground up. But he stayed small enough that he could give every job his personal attention. And for certain friends, he'd accept remodeling jobs—giving them the same degree of care. His partner, Vince Darden, mainly stayed in the office, but Victor liked the physical labor connected with being in the field. At certain times he ran two crews and would alternate between locations.

He wondered if he would be going to the reunion if it weren't for the job. He had wanted to ask Marion for a date, but lacked the courage. She sometimes left her shop and watched him and his crew work, offering advice or asking questions. Then one day she had brought him lunch in a basket, and they ate on the job. Another time she suggested they go eat at a fast-food place. And the funny thing, they had a lot to talk about. Finally, he asked to take her out to dinner and a movie. She accepted. That was really a sweaty-palm night, but he'd had a great time. Then, four days ago at the house, she had invited him to her high school reunion.

He pulled into the long circular drive and parked. The exterior of the house combined brick accents and cedar trim to give a rustic country feel. The sloping roof contained three dormer windows with enough space above them to allow large skylights for the studio. At one end was a huge brick chimney from ground past roofline. On the other end was an enclosed two-car garage and beyond that an iron fence comprised of eight-foot-high vertical rods connected by horizontal rods twenty-four inches from top and bottom. The vertical rods were ten inches apart. The previous owner had chosen that fence more for security than looks. Anyone climbing over could get spiked.

He got out of the door and approached the house. He had been there so much at work that it almost felt like going home. He rang the bell. The door opened immediately and there she stood. She was wearing a blue silk dress with a one-strand pearl necklace. Her pumps were dyed-to-match blue. Her face was accented on either side by pearl drop earrings.

"You look nice," she said, sensing he was having trouble speaking. "Will you help me with my coat?"

She handed him the coat and as she turned her back to him he had an impulse to forget the coat and hold her instead. Was he thirty-eight or eighteen?

"I really like your car," she said, settling back as though she were becoming part of the leather. Now he wanted to put the car in afterburner. Was he eighteen or sixteen?

Finally, he felt like he could talk. "You look beautiful," he said. She smiled. "I've got some seventies music," he added, pushing in an album. So while they drove across town to the Reston Hills High School gym they listened to a collection including "Delta Dawn," "Tie a Yellow Ribbon Round the Old Oak Tree," "How Deep is Your Love," "Lucille," and "You Are the Sunshine of My Life."

The first reaction he had to the reunion was related to the cars in the parking lot. He saw examples of BMW, Mercedes, Saab, Lexus, Infiniti, and Maxima. At least his car didn't feel like a castoff. But if anyone owned a Chevrolet, would he show up at this reunion? Or was the real purpose to parade success before old classmates?

Of course, there were some Chevrolets, Fords, and Plymouths in the lot. You just had to look for them.

Marion held his arm as they walked to the door. Inside came the ooh's and aah's. People swarmed and soon Marion was talking excitedly to a handful of women, introducing Victor to them.

"I'll get us some punch," Victor said.

Marion nodded, waving. Then she was talking again as Victor walked away. He wondered if she would go with him to his reunion—the twentieth would be coming up. Not at Reston Hills though— Jefferson Street High, much less upscale. There probably wouldn't be as many foreign cars.

He made his way to the punch bowl, nodding and smiling at every face that moved by, excusing himself for every shoulder he brushed against. A rock group was playing some of the oldies, mainly slow numbers at this early stage, and couples were dancing in the space between the platform and other standing groups who wanted nothing but shared memories and current gossip.

Marion looked glad to see him when he got back to her. She drank the punch and barely swallowed before she started talking. "Let me introduce you to . . ."

A sea of faces went by during various introductions throughout the evening, mixed with more dippings into the punch, more tasting the various servings of finger food, and more sitting down at an occasional table where Marion could spend longer times in catching up. At one such table a woman in a bright red dress hurried over and bent down and whispered in Marion's ear. Her face paled. She looked in a full circle around the room. A commotion to one side ended with a group separating as a man pushed through. He shuffled unsteadily.

"Hello, wife."

"What are you doing here?" Marion asked, her face aghast.

"You thought I was in Chicago, didn't you? But you didn't think I'd miss our class reunion, did you?" He stood wavering. Marion stood up, looking at Victor. "Let's go."

Victor moved with her, but the man caught her shoulder and whipped her around. "Don't run out on me. You did that once before. Ran out on our marriage. Took my son. My own father won't have anything to do with me. But I'm here to tell everyone what a phony you are."

Victor pushed him back. "That's enough."

The man focused on him, then looked at Marion. "Who's this guy?"

"You're drunk," she said, taking Victor's hand. "Let's go, Victor."

"Victor? Victor Borge? You a comedian?"

"Sit down." Victor motioned to a chair. "Right there. You'll feel better."

"How does this feel—?" The man swung a round-house right so wide that Victor could have read the sports section before it arrived. He put up his hand and caught the fist, holding it motionless. The man stood staring at Victor, who put his other hand on the man's forearm and forced him into the chair. He held him there, and after a moment the man looked around and said, "Anybody got a drink?"

Victor released him then. Marion took Victor's arm. "Please, let's go."

On the way home they both were silent. Finally Marion said, "I'm sorry."

"I'm sorry he bothered you."

"He went to Chicago years ago to live near his brother. I had no idea he might come back for the reunion."

"He's a nice-looking guy."

She glanced at him. "We were high school sweethearts. I'm afraid I thought too much about his looks."

"You were only eighteen."

"As he was. My parents tried to talk me out of the wedding. They wanted us to wait. So did his parents. But we were madly in love. His parents liked me and they doted on him. He was the baby in the family."

"Didn't he want to go to college?"

"He wanted to go right to work, and his father had connections to get him a job selling real estate."

When they pulled up in her drive she said, "I'd invite you in, but I'm afraid I wouldn't be good company. I'd like you to come back when you can spend some time with Jerry."

"I'd like that," Victor said. "He's a fine boy."

"He likes you, too. I think he wants to be a building contractor when he grows up."

Victor smiled and then turned serious. "Marion, I want to say something. I had a happy marriage, and I haven't been attracted to any woman since Paula died. I'm not a kid anymore, but right now I feel like a kid. And you're the reason. And if I'm going too fast, then I'm sorry. But I want to see you again, on a personal level. And if I do, it will be because I'm looking for a serious relationship. If you don't feel the same way, it's better we deal with each other only professionally. But I think I could fall in love with you." He smiled. "In fact, I think I've already started to."

Her eyes seemed to soften as she looked at him. She laughed. "That's a pretty good speech, Victor." She took his hand. "Of course I want to see you again. Do you think I would have invited you to my high school reunion if I weren't thinking serious thoughts about you? Dear man, we've know each other a long time, and I've seen you married to a woman you loved. I think I have a pretty good idea what kind of a husband you'd make. I'm a business-woman. You think I don't know how to add up a ledger?"

His heart was pounding and there wasn't anything on earth that he could think of to say or do.

"Are you going to kiss me good-night or make another speech?" she asked.

Now he knew exactly what to do.

His brother was watching a rerun of *"The Avengers"* on cable when he got home, propped up on the sofa and holding a half-full bottle of Zima. "How'd it go?" he asked.

Victor hung his coat in the closet and turned to him. "Can we kill the TV, Mike?"

"Sure." Mike clicked off the remote. Victor sat in a nearby chair and leaned toward him.

"Vince complained about you again today."

"Your partner is always complaining."

"What's with you and Faye White?"

Mike shrugged. "I date her some."

"She's only nineteen."

"That makes it legal."

"What does that mean?"

"She's legal, man—for anything."

Victor reached forward and grabbed Mike's shirt, jerking him forward so their faces were six inches apart. "Listen—before Mom died I promised her I'd take care of you, but I can't live your life for you. I'm tired of cleaning up your tracks after you've walked into someone's house from a muddy field. It's time you grew up or got out."

"Hey, I didn't mean anything. Faye's just a kid. I've only dated her a couple of times."

Victor released his shirt. "Harold White is a close friend of Vince. He doesn't want you seeing his daughter."

"I know she's too young. I met her at a bar when she was with a friend."

"Mike, you're working for our company because you're my brother. Vince won't even talk to you. You're just about out of chances."

"I do good work."

"When you're there. You know how many times you've been sick the past month?"

"I can't help when I'm sick."

"You can help not being out late the night before an early day. I've asked myself why, Mike. You've always been different—on the edge. You've rebelled against almost everything most people consider worthwhile. You didn't get any of that attitude from Mom and Dad, and you didn't get it from me."

"All I saw in you was Mr. Model Son, Mr. Conformity, Mr. Churchgoer, Mr. Straight."

Victor stared at him, then slowly shook his head. "Mike, you've lived in more places than I know about; you've been fired from jobs for not showing up; you've been in bar fights; you've been arrested for being drunk and disorderly. The last time you were arrested the judge listened to me when I said you could live here, that I would give you a job. But I did that because you made me a promise. Do you remember?"

Mike nodded. "I've kept that promise."

"We agreed you'd consider this a time of probation."

"But I need some freedom."

"I haven't tried to make this a jail. I haven't tried to keep you from going out or made you adhere to a curfew. You're thirty-five years old! All I want is for you to settle down, find some sense of stability. I want you to live your own life, but one that you can be proud of. That's all Mom and Dad would want."

"I never could be what they wanted."

"Come to church with me Sunday."

"You think that will help?" Mike stood up and moved around the room. "I got enough of that when we were kids." He moved to a picture on the wall of Sallman's *Head of Christ*. "Mom had this picture right above the kitchen table." He turned to Victor. "What ever happened to that other picture she had, where Jacob was wrestling with an angel?"

"It's in a trunk somewhere."

"Imagine wrestling with an angel?" Mike laughed. "Now that's some thought. I wonder how Hulk Hogan would have done with him?"

"Let's get back to the subject."

"Angels *are* the subject. If you're talking about church, you might as well be talking about angels and all that other stuff in the Bible." Mike moved back and sat on the sofa. "I'll tell you what, dear Brother. You want me to change. OK—here's the deal. Show me an angel. Show me something that an angel does. I mean—something I can see. If I really see something—with no doubts in my mind—I'll be Mr. Churchgoer. I'll be Mr. Straight. No more all-nighters. No more booze—" he hesitated, "—a little beer, maybe. But you know what I'm saying. I'll become so good I can move out of here and you can stop worrying about me."

Victor looked at him a long time. "You think all this is funny, don't you?"

"I'm serious," Mike said, but he couldn't stop the grin.

"And I'm serious," Victor said. "This is going to be my last talk to you. If you can't straighten yourself out, whether you believe in angels or anything else, it's time for us to check with the judge and you to move on."

In bed that night Victor thought back over what he had said to Mike. He wasn't about to abandon his brother. He had made a promise to his mother, but more than that, he loved his brother. He just didn't know if he could help his brother. Time would tell.

Then he thought about Marion and the same words surfaced again. Time would tell. But he had a more optimistic feeling about her.

The next day Victor checked the weather forecast. Rain was still not expected so he'd keep his schedule of starting the roof today. The shingles had already been delivered to the house and were under cover.

He'd have four men working today, including Mike and himself.

He arrived at the house with his men before Marion left for work. In fact, she was in her house-robe seeing her son rush out the door heading for the school bus stop. "Hey, Jerry," Victor yelled. The boy waved back and took off running. He had to go two blocks for the pickup point.

Marion was still standing in the door as Victor approached.

"Good morning," she said.

Victor spoke quietly so the men couldn't hear. "I thought you were beautiful last night. But you're more beautiful now."

"Sure." She smiled. "Morning light, no makeup. I look great."

"You just don't know how great."

She made a face. "Want some coffee?"

"Let me get the guys started. We're going to work on the roof today."

"Come on to the kitchen."

Victor had two ladders placed—one near the driveway end and one closer toward the middle in front. After a few instructions to the men he turned to the door.

"What about me?" Mike was grinning. "Can I have some coffee, too?"

"Behave," Victor said, not looking back.

She was sitting at the table holding a coffee cup. Near her was another cup already poured.

"This is a great way to start the day," he said, sitting.

"I like it."

He sipped. She sipped.

"Hot," he said. She nodded.

Silence. He realized he didn't have to talk to this woman. It was enough just to be near her. He could get used to this. He could get used to seeing her every morning and sitting with her and drinking coffee. Saying nothing, and knowing that his enjoyment of the silence said everything.

Later he watched her car drive away and stared after it all the way down the block until it disappeared around the corner.

"Brother, you've got it bad," Mike said.

"I've got it good."

"More power to you. But listen, if you ever marry that woman and move in here, tear up that mean-looking fence."

"I'd like to."

The four men began to cover the roof with shingles and by midmorning a good start had been made on the front. When they took a break Victor moved slowly around the house looking under the eave until he stood looking up at one end. He walked to the nearest ladder and called to Mike, "How about helping me move this ladder?"

"What's the matter?"

"I want to see if that's some rotten wood under the eave over there."

The two men carried the ladder to the driveway end and propped the ladder against the house. Victor started to climb, and Mike moved away, sitting where he could lean back against a tree. Victor was moving his hand over some wood. Then he looked and reached farther back toward the outer rim of the eave, bending slightly backward.

"Hey!" Mike yelled, "Be careful."

"I think we've got a little problem here."

"That ladder's the problem. Don't fall—"

Then it happened. Victor made one more stretch backward and the ladder began to go. He struggled to regain his balance. Mike jumped up but knew he would be too late. He was running forward but the ladder was already going, and Victor with it. Mike watched in horror. Victor was falling on his back straight toward the fence rods.

Mike yelled again. And then—what he saw he couldn't believe. Right before Victor hit the tips of the rods his direction changed in midair. His body shifted to the inside of the fence and then landed on the concrete driveway. It appeared that some invisible arms had caught his body and laid it on the ground. Mike ran to Victor, who was sitting up.

"What happened?" Victor said.

"Did you feel anything?" Mike asked.

"I don't know what happened. I know I was falling, but then I was on the ground."

"Are you hurt? Is anything broken?"

"I'm all right."

"No pain at all? Your back, your head?"

Victor shook his head. "No." He stood up.

"Are you still carrying Paula's angel?" Mike asked.

"Yes."

"I think—this time—the angel carried you."

Victor was touching his chest, his back, and still looking perplexedly at the fallen ladder. The other two men were staring at him.

Mike grabbed Victor's shoulder to get his attention. "Brother—"

Victor looked at him.

"I may go to church with you next Sunday," he said.

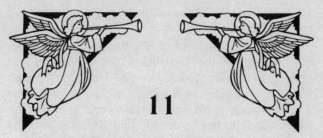

11

Duane's Angel

*Bless the Lord, all his angels, creatures of might
who do his bidding*

—PSALMS 103:20

Duane Green was in good position to break 200. He rarely did this, his league bowling average being 167. But tonight—he felt good. Not that a 200 would mean much to his team or league standing. This was a Friday night fun game with his best friend Teddy Kern. "Fun" was the operative word, gaining extra dimension because Cindy was working tonight. He enjoyed looking at her behind the refreshment counter. After a roll he always glanced in her direction, and after a strike he'd hold up circled fingers hoping to catch her attention. She did her share of smiling back.

Tonight Teddy was aware of the looks Duane gave Cindy, of course, but Duane's son Jack was too young to notice. Duane took Jack with him on Wednesday nights so that Velma could go out with her girlfriends. Velma called this her "Howling

Night," when she ate out with three old friends from her high school days.

Duane was proud of her. She had worked up to being manager of the Top Pick Video Store, and was making more money than he was. That didn't bother him. He was glad for the income. The old idea that a man should wear the pants—well, he wore the pants, all right, but he didn't mind a woman wearing pants. This was a different world from his father's day.

So why was he flirting with Cindy? Why did he look forward to seeing her? Why did he think about her when he was working on the carburetor of Mr. Gilmer's '87 Ford or was flushing out the radiator of Mrs. Jackson's '85 Buick? And why had he been attracted to Becky before Cindy, and Eunice before that?

Sure, he was only thirty-two, with muscles toned hard by manual labor and weight lifting. He could still turn the heads just like he did when he was flanker back at Wilmington High and All-State his senior year. There were a lot of girls then and there could be now. Except he was married and had a six-year-old son.

Still, the old potential was in place. He had been called a jock and a stud, and neither sobriquet insulted him. He took inner pride when someone else mirrored his own opinion.

The first few years of married life he had barely noticed another woman. Velma was a looker, and he had no reason to gaze elsewhere. He still had no reason, but when he turned thirty his self-image changed. He didn't *feel* any older, but he could see a couple of gray hairs at his temples and a few lines starting to cross his forehead. He didn't want to get old.

He remembered how he used to laugh at old people. Old Man Granger on Maple Street—Duane would see him most every morning walking his dog. He hobbled like he was afraid his legs would give way, while the Lhasa apso tugging on his lead would yap yap at the slowing school bus with its squealing brakes. Duane had never liked that Lhasa, but the thing he disliked the most was the way Old Man Granger walked.

Eunice had bowled a lot with her boyfriend. Duane appreciated the way she filled out sweaters—she had lots of sweaters. She couldn't be more than eighteen, and Duane wasn't about to make any moves on her. But he noticed her plenty, even introducing himself and striking up a conversation every chance he got.

Becky was older. He had first noticed her on League Night. She bowled with Rogers' Rebelettes, representing Rogers' Greenhouse and Gift Shop. They wore short yellow skirts and red jackets, and she had a custom green ball. He introduced himself to her, too, and went with her a couple of times for a beer at Cowan's Pub near Lakeland Park.

Then came Cindy, and he forgot all about Becky. He spotted her the first night she started working at Southside Lanes. She had to be one of the best-looking women he had ever seen. Long brown hair, naturally wavy, with huge eyebrows and big full lips. Terrific figure. So what was she doing working here?

He bought coffee from her, and over the next few weeks got to know her through a number of conversations at the counter. One night he invited her out for late drinks and she accepted.

When Duane took Cindy through the door at Cowan's that night he realized he was feeling a little guilty. He hadn't felt that way when he brought Becky here. Why with Cindy?

After their beers came, Duane had leaned over and said, "You know I'm married, don't you?"

She smiled. "How would I know that?"

"You've seen me with my son on Wednesdays."

She shrugged. He said, "You never asked me about him."

"Not my business."

"You don't mind I'm married?" he asked. "You go out with a lot of married guys?"

She lighted a cigarette. "Look," she said, "if you're trying to bring up morality, talk to yourself."

"I was just curious."

"Why don't you bring your wife here?"

"She wouldn't come."

"Why not?"

"She doesn't drink."

"Sounds admirable."

He nodded. "She's a good woman. Maybe too good." He stared at his mug, twisting it slowly around. "Sometimes I wish she were like she was before we got married. We went to a lot of places, did a lot of things. We were on the same wavelength. And we still are. Except, when Jack was born, not long after, she got converted in a Baptist revival. She doesn't mind me having a drink now and then, but she won't go anyplace like this with me."

Cindy stubbed out her cigarette. "I'd hang on to her. A good woman is hard to find."

"What about you?" he asked. "Are you married?"

"No."

"Where are you from?"

She took a drink from her mug. "Cincinnati."

"A long way off."

"My sister lives here."

She was silent a moment, and he said, "You look like a model. It's unusual to see someone like you working at Southside Lanes."

"My sister's a friend of the owner's wife." She took another drink, and started talking about her past. She had wanted to be a photographer's model, but had been told her endowments were overly abundant for fashion photography. They wanted her to do swimwear and lingerie. But after a couple of shoots she discovered that the action desired was more than getting in front of a camera. So she quit photography, and landed some showroom and platform work. And Lex landed her.

His favorite axiom? "Lex rhymes with sex."

But Lex was a handsome, slick-talking, flashy-dressed, take-charge guy who had her saying yes before she even knew the question. In living with him, she learned what hell was like.

"I stayed with him too long," she said. She ordered another mug of beer and laughed brokenly.

"I'm here to recover, to put the pieces back together. And avoid any serious entanglements."

She looked at him then. "Yes, I knew you were married. That's why I don't mind going out with you. Because you and I are going nowhere. We can be friends, if you can be content with that. I need someone to talk to besides my sister. But no guys who are free and available. Not now, not for a long time."

So after the first night Duane didn't feel guilty about Cindy anymore. The sexual attraction was still there, but with Cindy setting the boundaries he no longer felt the tension. He looked forward to seeing her; he thought about her; he was stimulated by her presence; but their glances at each other and secret smiles were only spice that added a little adventure to ordinary daily life.

His two nights of bowling followed a formula. Wednesday nights with Jack present he only got a couple of conversations with Cindy while he bought Cokes. On Friday nights, his League Night, he made more visits to the counter and then waited until closing to take her to Cowan's. They talked, laughed, and sometimes held hands. She shared in his glory days on the football field. He felt her excitement the first time she stood backstage with a dresser making last-minute preparations to her gown right before she moved out onto the platform. When he drove her home she never lingered in the car, nor invited him in to meet her sister.

On this night when Duane was heading for 200, he knew one more strike could lead to his all-time highest score. Striking in the tenth frame would then give him two more balls, and if he could strike those, he'd end up with 227. He glanced one more time in Cindy's direction to see if she were watching, and moved deliberately to get his ball and face the pin deck. He owned a blue ball that weighed sixteen pounds. Unlike most balls, which had three holes drilled for fingers, Duane had specified only two holes. The other unusual aspect of his game was his three-step delivery rather than the normal four-step. He concentrated on a spot between the number 1 pin and the number 3 pin. Then he made his quick approach and released the ball so that there was hardly a sound of contact between ball and floor. The ball rolled at high speed and then began to hook, hitting between the 1 and 3 and sending the other pins cascading in all directions.

Strike!

Teddy let out a yell. Cindy was smiling. Two more shots. And Duane no longer had any doubts. He knew he would get strikes.

He did.

"Great game," Teddy said. Other team members congratulated Duane. "Beer at Cowan's?" Teddy asked.

"Later," Duane said.

Teddy raised his eyebrows. "Cindy again? Better watch it, pal."

"I told you, just friends."

Teddy wasn't buying it. "Sure." He moved away and Duane went to the counter.

"My personal best," he said. Cindy was taking off her apron.

"Let's go."

"Aren't you closing?"

"I asked Nate to get off early. Anyway, this is my last Friday night."

Cindy was unusually quiet on their way to Cowan's. Duane wanted to talk about his game, but something in her attitude kept him quiet.

At Cowan's the change was still evident. Usually they talked freely with lots of laughs. Tonight she seemed preoccupied.

"What's this about not working Friday nights?" he asked.

"I'm taking Fridays off from now on," she said. "You won't have to wait till closing to see me."

"I always see you before closing."

"I mean we can come here earlier when I'm not working. Anyway," she said, looking at him sharply, "wouldn't your wife like you to get home earlier?"

"Velma understands about Friday nights. She has her night out; I have mine."

"Does she know what you do?"

"She knows I bowl, and that I come to Cowan's and relax."

She grinned thinly. "Just another night with the boys."

After that they didn't talk more until he suggested they dance. She shook her head.

"Let's go. I need to get home."

In the car they didn't speak. He had no idea what was wrong, but he didn't want to ask. When he pulled up in front of her house Cindy hesitated before getting out. She sat there looking at the dash, her hand on the door handle.

"What's the matter?" Duane finally said.

She looked up at him. "My sister thinks I should stop seeing you."

"Why?"

"She doesn't think it's—healthy."

"Doesn't she know we're just friends?"

"She doesn't think a man and a woman can stay friends."

"But that's all we are."

She didn't speak for a moment. "She says if you loved your wife, you wouldn't want to keep seeing me."

"Didn't you once tell me that my wife was my problem? That if I felt comfortable seeing you, then you weren't going to worry about it?"

She nodded.

"Then what's the problem?"

She stared at him for a long moment. Without warning she leaned forward and pressed her mouth hard against his and he felt jolted by a charge of electricity. Then she drew away from him and quickly got out of the car before he could move or say anything. He watched her run toward the house, and he was still unable to move. Slowly, then, he put the car in gear and drove away, his mind racing far faster than the echoing sound of his accelerating engine.

At home Velma was sitting up in bed reading. "You're home early. How'd you do?"

"My highest score—227."

She nodded. "I wish you would check on Jack. He's been coughing, and was running a fever this afternoon. I gave him some aspirin."

Duane moved down the hall to Jack's bedroom. A night-light was on, and Duane could see Jack breathing fitfully in his sleep. He moved to Jack, feeling his forehead. Hot. He went back to his bedroom.

"I think he's still got a fever. Did you check his temperature tonight?"

Velma nodded. "It was 101."

"I think he's hotter than that. I'm going to wake him."

"I wish you wouldn't. He had trouble getting to sleep."

"I want to check his fever."

He got the thermometer and gently shook Jack's shoulder. Velma came and stood in the doorway.

Jack muttered and opened his eyes. "Dad, what's the matter?"

"Let's check your temperature." He put the thermometer under Jack's tongue. Velma came over and felt Jack's head.

"He does seem hotter than he was."

The thermometer said 102.8. "Let's give him some more aspirin," Duane said.

"I'm thirsty," Jack said, coughing.

Duane gave him two aspirin and Jack drank greedily. "Can I have some more water?" he asked. Duane refilled the glass. After Jack finished Duane carefully tucked him under the cover.

"I don't want the cover," Jack said.

"It's too cold. You keep your cover on." Duane patted his shoulder.

Back in their bedroom Duane said, "If he still has the fever tomorrow, we'd better take him in."

Velma nodded. "The flu's going around. Emma was in bed all day Thursday. She called me today and started coughing so bad she had to quit talking."

Duane grinned. "That must have been hard on her."

"She sounded miserable."

"I'm sorry she's sick."

After he was in bed with the lights out, he lay with his hands behind his head, reliving the startling moment of Cindy's kiss. That kiss changed everything. And the irony was he had done nothing—no advances, no lines, no innuendos. He liked Cindy, and sure, the fact she was beautiful didn't dampen his interest in seeing her. But she had laid down the ground rules, and their relationship had been strictly talk and laughs. He could always talk to Teddy, but talking to Cindy was more stimulating. Maybe the sex thing did make the difference. He enjoyed talking to a woman. He couldn't talk to Velma that way anymore. She wouldn't go to bars or even dance. It was like they each had their own lives. It felt good at thirty-two to know he could still attract a beautiful woman. So with Cindy he had been having the best of two worlds, without having to feel guilty.

Until tonight. That kiss pointed to truckloads of future guilt, and grief. And so the decision was no contest. He loved Velma and his son, and nothing would be allowed to jeopardize his role as husband and father.

"Duane," his wife said softly.

"Eh?"

"Can't you sleep?"

"How did you know I wasn't sleeping?"

"You weren't moving."

"You mean I wiggle when I sleep?"

"You turn from side to side when you first get into bed, until you get comfortable and drop off."

"I'm just not sleepy."

"Thinking about your game?"

"Yeah."

"I wish I could have seen it."

"You could have."

"Friday is your night with the boys."

"We don't do much together anymore."

Silence. Then after a moment. "I'm sorry, Duane. I'm just so tired every night. I'm always shorthanded at the store."

"We could go out on Saturday night."

"We've discussed that."

"I know, I know. You can't stay up late because of church the next day."

"We could go to church together."

Now he was silent. "Let's not argue about that."

"But Jack enjoys Sunday School. And at church he looks around and sees other boys with their fathers and he wants you to be with him."

"I don't like church. You knew that when you married me."

"But things are different now."

"Because of Jack? Look, I don't mind your filling his head with the Bible. Teach him about miracles and angels and all the rest, but leave me out of it. My mother hammered church at me enough to last a lifetime."

"All right, Duane," she said, "but I pray for you every night."

"So did my mother," Duane said sarcastically.

After that Velma turned on her other side and fell silent. Duane closed his eyes, but his thoughts kept returning to Cindy and the feel of her lips. He drifted into sleep, his dreams taking over his thoughts but now the setting was changed from his car to an airplane. He was flying with Cindy in a private plane over the mountains, with Cindy excitedly pointing out the breathtaking vistas far below. Suddenly she turned from the window and grabbed him, kissing him as he forgot to control the plane. The plane started downward, but she kept her lips on his. He tried to break away as the windshield broke and cold wind slapped against him. He finally broke away but it was too late. The plane was hurtling downward toward a wall of snow, and the cold air numbed him right before the crash.

At the crash his eyes opened. The cover had been piled to one side and he was cold. He reached to pull it back over him when he heard the cough. He listened, and then he heard it again. He got out of bed and went to Jack's room. Jack was sitting on the side of his bed, still coughing.

"Hey, it's too cold to be out of your cover."

"I'm hot."

Duane felt his head. "I'm going to check the temperature again."

By the time he put the thermometer into Jack's mouth, Velma had joined him. He looked at the thermometer. 103.1. "Let's give him some more aspirin," he said.

After Jack took the aspirin, Duane pulled the cover back over him. "You're going to the doctor tomorrow."

"I'll be all right," Jack said.

"You're going."

"I don't want to go to the doctor."

"You know you like Dr. Hudlow."

Jack made a face. "Will he give me a shot?"

"I don't know."

"I'm not going to have a fever tomorrow. You'll see."

Back in bed Duane said, "He never gets sick."

"It's got to be the flu," Velma said.

"I probably shouldn't have taken him with me Wednesday night."

"He could catch the flu anywhere."

"But he wasn't feeling too good that night. I should have stayed home."

"I didn't have to go out with the girls."

He adjusted the covers closer around his neck. "You work hard. You need that night out. I don't have to go bowling on Wednesdays. League Night's enough."

"Jack likes going bowling with you," Velma said. "He likes being with his father."

"We can do other things." He looked at the dark ceiling, and then in a voice so soft she could hardly hear, "I really love that kid."

The next morning they checked Jack's temperature before he got out of bed. Almost normal.

"I told you I wouldn't have a fever," Jack said.

"I know," Duane said, looking at the thermometer and feeling relieved.

"Mom, can I have pancakes?"

Velma smiled. "OK."

"Can I go over to Andy's house this afternoon?"

"I think you'd better stay in."

"I'm not sick."

"You still have a little fever."

After breakfast Duane pushed back his plate. "The pancakes and eggs were great, Velma."

"Yeah, Mom. But why can't we have pancakes on other days besides Saturdays?"

"Because Saturday is the one day we aren't rushed."

"We could have them on Sunday."

She smiled. "If we got up early enough. But it seems we always have to rush to get to church on time."

"Maybe Dad could make the pancakes while you're getting ready," Jack said, "since he doesn't go to church."

Velma glanced at Duane, who in turned looked at Jack. "Maybe I will one of these times."

"You'll make pancakes?" Jack asked.

Duane grinned and shook his head. "No—go to church."

"Dad, you ought to go. You learn about all kinds of neat stuff, like last Sunday when the preacher was telling about how an angel got Peter out of prison. He said the angel made the chains fall off Peter and then the angel opened the locked doors and led Peter away from prison. Remember, Mom?"

She nodded.

Jack went on. "But it was funny what the preacher said, about Peter not knowing if it were real. He said Peter thought he was seeing a vision. Why wouldn't Peter know if the angel were real?"

"I don't know much about angels," Duane said, "but some people have dreams and they think they see angels. Maybe Peter had a dream."

"But, Dad—Peter got out of prison. The angel had to be real."

Duane shrugged. "Maybe he was."

"Angels could be in dreams and still be real, couldn't they?"

Duane gave a perplexed look at Velma. She smiled, "Maybe Daddy would know more about angels if he did start going to church."

Duane looked at his watch. "I need to get to the garage and work on Mr. Macklin's transmission. He needs the car back Monday." He kissed Jack, and then moved to Velma. As he bent to kiss her he had a sudden vision of another face, and the kiss he gave Velma was light and quick.

He worked all morning on the transmission, but his mind kept returning to the night before and the feel of Cindy's lips. Then close to noon he washed up and made a phone call. He recognized her voice.

"Cindy?"

"Yes. —Duane?"

"I'm having to work at the garage this morning."

"Overtime, eh?"

"A promise to a friend." Then neither said anything, and the silence stretched into an epoch. Finally he got out the words. "About last night—"

Another silence. This time her voice came first. "About last night—?"

"The night ended—funny."

"I'm afraid I lost control," she said.

"Me, too."

"So where does that leave us?"

"Where do you want it to leave us?"

"I don't know."

"The thing is," he said, "that kiss moved us someplace different. And that's not—where I want to be."

"Oh?" Her voice was small.

"You gave us our location at the beginning—a place called Friendship. I got comfortable living there. But I'm afraid that kiss was a ticket out of town."

"And you don't want to ride the bus to a new place?"

"I like the old place," he said, "and I think the bus had better go without me."

She didn't reply immediately, and he waited anxiously. Finally she said, "I understand."

"Good-bye," he said. She said nothing, and he waited until he heard the click of the phone before hanging up.

By midafternoon he was almost finished when the phone rang. He hoped it wasn't Cindy.

"He's running a fever again." Velma's voice was distraught.

"How high?"

"Nearly 104."

"Did you call Dr. Hudlow?"

"I'm taking Jack to his office. Can you meet me?"

"I'll see you there."

Duane was more worried than he wanted to be. While driving, he thought back on the times when Jack had run a fever. When he was very young he could bounce to 104 and back down with alarming suddenness and yet seemingly with no lasting effects. But Jack wasn't a baby anymore, and he never got sick, and 104 could mean bad news.

The doctor's attitude didn't give him relief. After examining the boy, Dr. Hudlow said, "I think we'd better put him in the hospital."

Duane couldn't believe it. "What's wrong with him."

"I'm not certain yet, but he has a severe respiratory tract infection."

"The flu?" Velma asked.

"Perhaps, but we need to keep an eye on him. I'd feel better if he were in the hospital."

"But he was feeling so good this morning," Velma said.

"You say he had a fever last night?"

"The first we noticed it."

"And he's been coughing?"

"Yes, but we gave him aspirin and he got to sleep and this morning felt much better."

Dr. Hudlow nodded. "Well, let me say first, no more aspirin. I thought I had told you, with any fever of unknown origin, take acetaminophen rather than aspirin."

"You think the aspirin hurt him?"

"We'll watch him carefully. Perhaps he can come home after a couple of days. I'll call the hospital and make the arrangements."

That night in the hospital Jack got horribly sick in his stomach. The next day he lay in bed and showed little enthusiasm for talking. His temperature had gone down, but Duane was disturbed by the way he looked. He seemed disoriented, unable to connect with questions, not responding to comments. Duane could see Velma's unspoken worry etched deeply in the lines around her mouth and eyes. The doctor could tell them nothing beyond saying that they were running tests. That night Duane stayed with Jack, trying to be as comfortable as possible in a cushioned chair by the bed.

At 2:20 Duane came awake from sporadic dozing to see Jack sitting up in bed. His face was elevated as though looking through the ceiling to a distant place far above. He was smiling, his head moving back and forth and his eyes changing direction as though focusing on wondrous sights. Duane moved quickly to him, touching his shoulder.

"Jack—"

Jack sank back to the pillow.

"Jack, are you all right?"

At that moment Jack seemed to notice Duane for the first time. "Hi, Dad."

"What is it, son?"

Jack closed his eyes for a moment, then opened them.

"Angels. I saw the angels."

"Where?"

"They were there, singing to me. Singing like the angels sang for the baby Jesus. I felt good."

Duane rubbed his hand over Jack's head. "You were dreaming."

Jack closed his eyes and seemed to drop off to

sleep. Duane watched him for a long moment. Then he sat back in the chair, and as he tried to doze, he wished that Jack did have angels looking after him, singing to him.

The next day Jack seemed even more lethargic and disoriented. He had trouble remembering things at home. The doctor spoke to Duane and Velma in the afternoon.

"The tests point to Reye's syndrome."

"What's that?" Duane asked.

"It's relatively rare, characterized by brain dysfunction and sometimes liver damage. I haven't seen any sign of a liver problem with Jack. The syndrome develops with symptoms we've observed—vomiting, lethargy, memory loss, disorientation."

"What causes it?"

"It follows a respiratory tract infection, such as flu or chicken pox. As I say, it's relatively rare."

"Then why did Jack get it?"

The doctor hesitated. "Sometimes Reye's syndrome is related to taking aspirin for a viral infection."

Duane was stunned. Velma looked as though she were about to cry. "But that doesn't happen often. This is an unusual case. We've got him on mannitol. If his liver does get damaged, we're equipped to put him on dialysis."

"Dr. Hudlow." Duane had trouble talking. "Are you saying Jack's life is in danger?"

Again the doctor hesitated. "To be honest, I have to say there's a chance he may not recover."

"How big a chance."

"I'd say about a ten percent chance. But that means a ninety percent chance he will recover." The doctor spoke encouragingly. "The picture is not nearly as grim as it used to be."

Velma spoke as though each word was as fragile as an eggshell. "You mean Jack could die?"

"The odds are against it, Mrs. Green. We'll just hope now that he won't have any seizures."

Jack had his first seizure that night. Velma was watching and she called the nurse in panic. Soon a doctor and other nurses were working with him. The next day the doctor was more solemn.

"He may slip into a coma," he said.

"What does that mean?" Duane asked.

"It means his heart rhythm may be disturbed. His breathing could be affected. And we have to be concerned that any serious attack could result in brain damage."

Duane and Velma looked hopelessly at each other. Duane put his arm around her and she began to sob.

During the day Jack opened his eyes and spoke rationally. "I saw them again," he said, "the angels, and they were sitting in a circle and they were asking me to join them."

Duane tried to smile. "Did they sing to you anymore?"

"Not this time."

"What do they look like?" Duane asked.

"Like us. Like people."

"How do you know they're angels?"

"Because they don't sound like us." Jack closed his eyes and his head relaxed on the pillow. Duane hoped he could keep Jack awake a while longer.

"How do they sound?"

Jack's lips moved slowly, as though speaking from

a great distance. "They have voices that sound sweet."

Duane watched his son breathing deeply, and reached out for Velma's hand. He felt her tightening grip.

Jack didn't regain consciousness the rest of the day. That night, full of fatigue, Duane stood up and went to the restroom. He stared in the mirror and splashed water in his face. As he was drying his face with a paper towel a man entered and began to wash his hands in the next lavatory. The man wore an orderly's white uniform and looked tired. After a moment Duane glanced at him.

"Rough night?" he asked.

"Not as rough as yours," the man replied.

"Are you familiar with my boy, in room 712?"

"I know him."

Duane had never seen the orderly, and was curious. "I don't remember seeing you."

The man smiled. "Your son has seen me."

"Did you see him today?"

"Yes. He was awake."

"He was awake once with us. But that was all. I guess he woke up when we were taking a lunch break in the cafeteria. You came by then? Is that when you saw him?"

The man nodded. "He saw me, and he doesn't want you to be afraid."

"He talked to you?"

"He wants you to know that he's going to be all right."

"Did he mention anything about angels?"

The man smiled. "No."

"He thinks he sees them. I'm glad he was able to see you, someone real."

"Do you read the Bible, Mr. Green?"

"Not much."

The orderly was drying his hands. "Disease is like a prison, and sometimes a miracle happens when the chains are parted and the cell door opens and the prisoner can walk forth into the greatest freedom he has ever known."

"My son mentioned the story about an angel who rescued Peter from prison. He heard the minister preaching on it."

The man looked solemnly at Duane. "Your son has a lot to tell you. You should listen." Then he left the room.

"Wait—!" Duane said, rushing to the door and opening it. The hallway was empty. At the far end he could see a doctor checking a chart at the nursing station. No orderly anywhere. Duane closed the door and leaned back against the wall. Something had bothered him about the orderly. That business about disease being like a prison. Was the man trying to say that Jack could be saved from the prison of disease—by an angel striking away the chains and opening the cell door, like he did for Peter?

A coincidence. It all was a coincidence. The orderly happened to have seen Jack when Duane was out of the room. Coincidence. Jack just happened to wake up to see the orderly. Coincidence. The orderly just happened to refer to the same Bible story that Jack had mentioned to his parents. Coincidence.

But there was something else that bothered Duane about the orderly. What was it? His voice. What had his voice sounded like? He couldn't remember. Low, high, husky, clear? He couldn't recall.

Sweet? A voice that sounded sweet? No—but Duane could not think of another adjective that could describe that voice. And suddenly Duane began laughing. He shouldn't be laughing when his son could die. But his son wasn't going to die! He knew it as certainly as he knew something else—he had seen an angel.

12

Bob's Angel

All at once an angel of the Lord stood there, and the cell was ablaze with light

—Acts 12:7

Bob Martin didn't believe in angels. Not even after some half-naked guy beat his head against the north wall of his WJFV-AM announcing booth one Sunday morning twenty-one years ago. But what happened eleven years after that—in 1982—made him think again about that rainy Sunday in 1971. Twice? Had he been visited twice by a guardian angel?

The Sunday AM shift—called the "Religious Ghetto" by his colleagues—was his since he was the newest, lowest-paid staffer. Sunday morning on the small kilowatt AM station in Jeffersville, Illinois, was a mix of syndicated and local live preaching and gospel singing plus a large amount of pleading for donation support. He had graduated that spring from his community junior college, and now planned to work a year and save money, while living at home, to finish up at Southern Illinois University. He wanted to

major in broadcasting, and figured this experience
would look good on a future résumé.

His father was recently retired as an office clerk at
the local Coke bottling plant, and Bob was on his
own not only to save money for college, but for paying off the 1963 Ford Fairlane he got from his friend
Norman Ross, who had graduated with him from
high school, and who already was at SIU.

When Bob started his announcing job two weeks
after finishing his sophomore year, he was quickly introduced to the vagaries of a small broadcasting operation. Everyone did more than one job, and besides
his on-air work, he functioned as "traffic manager"—
having to follow the next day's schedule in pulling
from file drawers the needed commercials and placing them into the books with the program intros. This
kept him working after sign off each day, Saturday
being his only day off. On Sundays he had to open
up the station at sunrise—he and the station's engineer, Bill Radley.

Here WJFV differed from many stations, which
hired announcers who handled both mike and equipment. When it began operations in 1947, WJFV followed the current technology that decreed a separate
control room from the announcer's booth. In this control room the engineer played the records and commercials as cued by the announcer. The station still
maintained this practice in 1971.

On a rainy Sunday in August, Bob Martin would
be glad about this.

Bob's mother had been a faithful Baptist all her
life, while his father had grown up a Methodist. Bob,
himself, had been a Baptist since he was nine. He
had heard about angels all his life. But he didn't think

about them much. To him, angels were a biblical curiosity. They were mentioned in both the Old and New Testaments, and Bob was aware they often appeared in dreams. They were messengers, but sometimes they carried out other commands of God—like the angel who kept Adam and Eve from reentering the Garden of Eden. How angels looked was an open question to Bob. Did they have wings? The Bible did not indicate this. But they could appear to resemble human beings, and even take solid material form, as did the angel who wrestled with Jacob.

But Bob's mother sometimes spoke of another function of angels—to protect the lives of those who faced severe danger. Bob knew that some people believed everyone had a guardian angel, and several of the Sunday morning preachers mentioned this as a fact. But these same preachers would also speak as strongly about the existence of demons, and Bob had more trouble with this idea. It seemed to him that demons were a residue of belief from more primitive and superstitious times. The Bible mentioned demons, of course, but Bob was willing to ascribe this to the then prevailing cultural worldview.

So Bob was negative on the concept of demons and neutral on angels that Sunday in August.

He had to force himself from bed when the alarm went off at five o'clock. A movie the night before— *The French Connection* (great)—with a new date (not great) had not been enough to keep him from reading in bed. Gene Hackman certainly deserved an Oscar for the movie. But his date—forget any Oscar. He didn't really mind that she had no knowledge of the fact that Lee Trevino had won the U.S. Open, or Canonero II the Kentucky Derby, or Baltimore the

Super Bowl. But all she could talk about was her planned trip to Orlando, when Disney World was scheduled to open in October. She had been to Disneyland twice, and she had read how Disney World would be bigger and better. She described every Disneyland show, event, and ride in great detail until he had tried out two questions of his own: Did she think Nixon was right in killing the SST supersonic transport, and was she glad the twenty-sixth amendment now established the voting age at eighteen? Somehow the serious stuff didn't generate much excitement, so he didn't ask her if she thought Dow Jones would break the one thousand barrier this year.

The upshot was that he had stayed up reading from *The Naked and the Dead* and thinking of Vietnam. Now he was still suffering from only three hours of sleep as he drove to the station located a mile outside of town. Not even his favorite song coming from a St. Louis station helped his feelings. To make matters worse, the rain was coming down so hard that his old wipers were taking the ten count. Bill Radley's black pickup truck was already in the parking lot. Bob turned off the radio at the final note of "How Can You Mend a Broken Heart," cut the engine, and slid out of the car, quickly opening up his umbrella. He raced toward the door and almost fell down when he splashed across a puddle near the entrance.

Bill was his usual happy self, which really depressed Bob today. Bill was an early-to-bed guy who rose with the sun to look over his fifteen acres on the Walnut Hill Road. And when the rooster crowed, it could always count on being accompanied by Bill's echoing whistle.

"I hate rain," Bob said.

"We need it." Bill was working with a dial.

"The forecast didn't predict this much rain today." Bob shook off his coat and pounded his feet on the entrance rug.

"What do they know?"

"Yeah. And we have to read what comes over that teletype."

By this time Bob was starting the coffee. "Did you hear the Cardinal game Friday night?"

"Through the seventh inning," Bill said. The equipment hummed as he threw switches. Bob stopped at the small room housing the teletype, looking under the heading of "Misc. Trivia" and discovering that on this date in 1848 a patent had been issued for the first dental chair, and the Panama Canal was officially opened on this day in 1914. Then he entered the announcer's booth and checked the logbook. The first scheduled program was a syndicated half-hour preaching show, and Bill was laying the record on the turntable. Bob sat down, facing the microphone and a small bulb centered at the base of the glass separating announcer from engineer.

"All set?" Bill asked. Bob nodded. The sound of the National Anthem flooded the room, as Bob silently glanced at the sign-on copy. Then the music ended, and the bulb lighted.

"Good morning, and welcome to another broadcast day of WJFV-AM, your one-thousand-watt clear channel station in Jeffersville, the heart of southern Illinois." Bob motioned to Bill, and the bulb went off as Bill started the turntable. Introductory music was followed by a recorded voice announcing the program's title, the name of the preacher, and the singing group performing the first song. Bob would be off-air for the next twenty-eight minutes thirty seconds. He stood up, leaving the room to check the coffee. The red light was on, and Bob poured a cup, ignoring the powdered cream and sugar. Then he moved to the engineer's booth, blowing on his cup. Bill never drank coffee.

"Is Ellen doing all right?" Bob asked.

"Yeah, but her back still hurts. She had to get up twice last night." Ellen was Bill's wife, and she had fallen off a ladder while picking peaches. "Lying down for a long time really gets to her."

"She still wearing the brace?"

"Except when she sleeps."

Bob moved away and looked out the front door. The rain was still heavy, and across the highway he could make out trees bending under the gusty wind. *No time even for ducks,* he thought.

"Hey, come here," Bill called. Bob went to the open door. "This guy's talking about angels again, like he did last week. You know Ellen believes this stuff?" Bob picked up on the voice:

. . . and God used his angels to minister to his faithful—to guide and protect them. Hagar had fled her mistress Sarai, and an angel came to her by a spring in the wilderness and told her to return and God would make of her descendants a great nation. God later promised Abraham that he would send an angel to guide Abraham's servant in finding a wife for Isaac. And Moses spoke to his people: "But when we cried to the Lord, He heard our voice and sent an angel and brought us out from Egypt" (Numbers 20:16).

When Jezebel threatened Elijah's life, he fled to the wilderness and slept under a juniper tree, wanting to die. And the Bible says: "And behold, there was an angel touching him, and he said to him, 'Arise, eat.' Then he looked and behold, there was at his head a bread cake baked on hot stones" (1 Kings 19:5–6). And then the great promise of God to all his followers, in Psalm 91: "For He will give His angels charge concerning you, to guard you in all your ways. They will bear you up in their hands, Lest you strike your foot against a stone." My friends, God's angels take care of all who believe in Him, to guide, to guard and protect us. A guardian angel for everyone. Do you believe it? He'll come when you need him. Sometimes in a dream, as an angel appeared to Joseph and warned him to take Mary and his baby and flee to Egypt. Sometimes in a more tangible way, as to Peter and other apostles who had been thrown into prison. "But an angel of the Lord during the night opened the gates of the prison, and taking them out he said, 'Go your way . . .'" (Acts 5:19–20). We have a guardian angel, each of us. He will protect us. He will take care of us, watch over us, and guide us in all things. Amen and Amen.

"Ellen's grandmother believes in angels, too," Bill said. "We had her over for dinner two days ago and she told us she saw one."

"You're kidding."

"In a dream. When she was in a hospital last year and almost died from pneumonia. She said she saw a winged warrior dressed in radiant white garments, and he was speaking not in any language but she understood every word he spoke."

"What did he say?"

"He told her this wasn't her time to die."

"Hadn't she ever mentioned that dream before?"

"She said the angel told her to keep it a secret. And she did. But at our house she said she wanted to tell someone before something else happened to her. And she's always been close to Ellen. It would be nice, wouldn't it?"

"What?"

"If there *were* an angel assigned to you? And no matter what you did it was there to protect or guide you."

Bob shook his head. "What about the people who die in automobile wrecks? Or in war? Where are their angels?"

"I don't know. Maybe we're not supposed to understand everything."

Bob was silent a moment. "I wish I had a guardian angel. But I'd have to see one myself before I'd believe it."

Halfway through the program five men—a local gospel quartet and pianist—came in, shaking the water off their umbrellas, and then grouped themselves around a microphone in the small adjoining studio. Bob introduced their half-hour program and following them next read some local church promos which led into another syndicated preaching program—this one an hour long. Bill was drinking a carton of orange juice as Bob moved to the front door. The rain was coming down heavy as ever, and the parking lot had accumulated two more puddles that looked like lakes. He took the latest issue of *Broadcasting* from the coffee table and walked back to the announcer's booth. Sitting at the desk, he began to turn the pages. He got caught up in an article describing how FM was taking over from AM in popularity when a movement behind the glass caught his attention. Someone was in the engineer's room with Bill.

At first Bob couldn't believe what he was seeing. A bare-chested man wearing white Jockey briefs and nothing else was standing and gesturing toward the announcer's booth. Bill was shaking his head. Suddenly the man lashed out with his right fist, and Bill crashed backward to the floor. That galvanized Bob, who rushed from the booth. He faced the man, who turned toward him.

"What's going on?" Bob shouted, still in shock. The man towered six inches over Bob, and looked like a longshoreman who had a fixation on weight lifting.

"I want to talk on the radio," the man said.

"You can't—"

"I want to talk right now!"

"No—" Bob said, aware that Bill was getting groggily to his feet. The man clenched his right hand and stepped toward Bob.

"You can talk!" Bill interrupted. The man turned back toward him. "You can talk. Look—" Bill pointed to the small bulb at the base of the glass partition. "When that bulb is on the mike is live. You can go into that room and talk."

The man nodded. "I have to tell people about God."

Bob played along. "You can go in and talk as long as you want."

The man grabbed Bob's arm. "You come with me." At this point Bob made eye contact with Bill, looking toward the phone. Bill would turn on the bulb without the mike being live, and while the man talked Bill could call the sheriff. Meantime, Bob wanted to keep the guy talking. He let the man lead him into the booth. Then the man sat behind the mike, still holding Bob's arm.

"Introduce me," he said.

"What's your name?" Bob asked.

"Just say I'm the Lord's messenger."

Feeling foolish and relieved at the same time, Bob bent down and motioned to Bill. The bulb came on. Then Bob said, "Ladies and gentlemen, let me introduce you to the Lord's messenger, who has something to say to you."

The man let go of Bob's arm then, moving the mike closer. Bob could see Bill through the glass as he bent down to one side of his desk and talked rapidly into the phone. The man started to get up, but Bob tried to distract him by pointing to the lighted bulb. Bill quickly put down the phone, and the man settled back. He began to speak:

"The Lord Jehovah is your God. You must worship him, for he made you just as he made the rain outside. It washes over you, cleansing your body with its purity as you feel the cool hand of God's holiness. It covers your face, your hands, your chest, your legs, dripping into puddles at your feet. It mats your hair and blinds your eyes to everything but his glory. It is the garment you wear—the only garment—and nothing blocks you from the touch of his eternal love. You are to stand naked before God. Right now. For you are unworthy to look into his face. You must bow down and kiss his feet. Humble yourself. As a worm you must crawl to God and beg his forgiveness. For he will destroy you in your sin and wickedness, as he did Sodom and Gomorrah. Bow down and kiss his feet! Now!" At that moment he stood, pushing back the chair, and turned toward Bob.

"Bow down and kiss his feet!" He pointed to his own feet. Bob stared at him. "Kiss his feet, now!" He hit Bob on the chest. "Kiss my feet!" Bob staggered backward, shaking his head. The man struck at Bob's midsection, and Bob bent over, unable to breathe. Then the man grabbed his ears and slammed his head back against the wall, hammering it again and again. Luckily the wall was cushioned for soundproofing. Bob pounded at the man's head, but the blows had no effect. The man pulled back his right fist as though he were about to launch a roundhouse when he suddenly froze. He dropped his hands. Bob took a step backward, his fists high, protecting his face. The man stood motionless.

"Put your hands behind your back," Bob said. To his surprise the man meekly obeyed. Bob stripped his belt from his pants and stepped behind the man, wrapping the belt around each wrist and then crossing the belt in a figure eight between the wrists before buckling it in the tightest hole. Then he took the man's elbow and led him to the reception area, setting him in a chair near the front door. Bill watched them nervously.

"You get hold of the sheriff?" Bob asked.

Bill nodded.

Bob glanced at his watch. "Twelve more minutes on the program. Nice he didn't mess up our station break."

They heard squealing brakes outside, and then the door opened as the sheriff and his deputy entered, yellow raincoats dripping over black rubber galoshes. They stared at the nearly naked form sitting calmly staring straight ahead.

"We had got another call," the sheriff said. "Some couple driving along the highway saw this guy walking and shouting in the rain. They were afraid to stop. He hurt you?"

"I spoke on the radio," the man blurted. "I told all the people about Jehovah. Everyone must bow to Jehovah. Everyone must kiss his feet."

"Why did you try to make me kiss your feet?" Bob asked.

"I am Jehovah's representative. Inasmuch as you do it to me, you do it to Jehovah."

"Sure," Bob said.

"You would have kissed my feet, too, if that man hadn't helped you."

Bob grinned and looked at Bill. "Thanks, Bill."

"Not him," the man said. "The other man. The man with the sword."

"What are you talking about?"

"The man who came into the room. I was about to make you kiss my feet, and he came into the room with the sword. I wouldn't have let you tie my wrists if he hadn't been there with his sword. I'm not crazy."

"I'm glad you're not crazy," Bill said drily. The sheriff made the man stand, taking the belt off and putting on handcuffs. He handed the belt back to Bob.

"Sounds to me like you're lucky. We'll take care

of him. And thanks." He and the deputy led the man out.

"It was an angel," Bill said, grinning.

"What?"

"Your guardian angel. The guy saw him. He had a sword and protected you."

"Why didn't *I* see him, or you?"

"Maybe they only appear to those who *need* to see them. And think of the coincidence. That preacher talks about angels, and then this guy sees one who protects you."

"A *crazy* guy sees one."

During the following years Bob never forgot that rainy Sunday, but he credited his guardian angel to the imagined ravings of a disordered mind. The man had been a patient at the institution in Anna, and had escaped the day before. But eleven years later, on a day in October, something would happen that changed Bob's thinking forever.

After graduating from SIU in 1974, Bob had received offers from three stations in the Midwest. He took his first job in Springfield, Illinois. At first handling news and general announcing work, he bridged into being a disc jockey. The station manager told him he had the personality and voice to grab a youth audience. This eventually established him as a local air celebrity. One of the competing stations secretly taped him and sent his "audition" to various other markets. An overture from a Southern FM station was too good to pass up, and Bob moved south in 1979. His new station was rated #2 nighttime, but had moved to #1 in the three years since Bob took the premidnight shift.

Actually, Bob was not a great fan of the pop music

of 1982. A few exceptions, of course. He liked the
sentiment of "Ebony and Ivory" and the great mood
of "Chariots of Fire."

Five days a week Bob arrived at the station about
4:00 P.M. to prepare his broadcast. The work hours
didn't do much for his love life, limiting his serious
dating to two nights a week. But he liked his schedule. He spent a good two hours a day at the gym,
working out and jogging. The free daylight hours
suited him, and in any case he had a late lunch practically every day with Penny Edwards.

Penny was a talk show personality with a daily
morning three-hour shift on an AM station. Her bias
was left-of-center, and so were most of her phone
callers. President Reagan was a favorite target. She
didn't like the way movie production put people's
lives at risk (Vic Morrow and two children were
killed), or the money spent on the space shuttle that
could better be used on earth (Challenger was in
Florida getting ready for its first commercial flight),
or capital punishment (Charlie Brooks was scheduled
to be executed by lethal injection). Bob disagreed
with most of her opinions, but that didn't alter the
way he felt about her. She was twenty-seven, gorgeous, with a quick mind and strong feminist lean-
ings. Although he was four years older, he sometimes
felt she was the more experienced one. In one way
she was, being divorced from a former radio production director who became an alcoholic. But for some
reason Bob and Penny hit it off on first meeting—at
Jeb Reinhard's birthday party for his wife. Jeb was
Bob's station manager, with many friends throughout
the radio fraternity. Penny was close to his wife,
Helen.

"I don't want to do it," Bob said for the third time during lunch with Penny. The waitress poured him more tea and he took a drink. Even the tea tasted different here. Everything tasted different at *Good Life's*. Bob never enjoyed coming here, but Penny did. Organic health food—no meat whatever.

"Halloween is my favorite holiday, but I don't want to broadcast from Club 242."

Penny smiled. "You did it last year."

"And you know the trouble I had. The drunk guy who got past security and wanted to dedicate a song to his wife."

"He ended up singing to the police."

"The club doesn't sell drinks, but that doesn't stop people from coming in who have been drinking. There's something about Halloween that makes people wild, anyway."

"Then don't do it," Penny said.

"Yeah, sure. The remote is booked solid with advertisers who were given special deals. I tried to get Al to forget the whole thing, but Jeb backed him."

Penny cut into a green and yellow mix of vegetables that looked to Bob like imports from an alien world.

"Ken Bradley could do the remote," Bob continued, "but they won't let me off the hook."

"You're a victim of your own popularity, Bob. The advertisers want you."

Bob shook his head. "I don't like the place. Too many people can crowd in there. And it may not be safe."

"What do you mean?"

"The building is old."

"It's passed safety standards, hasn't it?"

"Yeah. But I still have a bad feeling."

Penny smiled coyly. "I'll be there."

Bob took her hand. "I know. And that's the only good thing about the remote. But I wish we could be somewhere else, alone."

Penny squeezed his hand. "Me, too. But I'll be taping comments for my own show on how people feel about Halloween. Every year calls come in from people who think Halloween is evil, that its observance glorifies demons and the devil. But most people understand it's simply a fun time. There's no need to make it a religious controversy."

Bob grinned. "But you'll make it a controversy on your show."

She nodded. "That's the idea of a talk show." She stared at Bob a moment. "You know, it's strange how well we get along. We don't agree on anything politically. We don't even like the same foods."

Bob lowered his voice. "Penny, have you done any more thinking about what we talked about Saturday?"

"About what?"

"About us. I know how you feel about marriage. But I also know how I feel about you. And I'm getting tired of being alone."

"Beginning to feel your age?"

"All thirty-one years of it."

She quickly patted his hand before withdrawing hers. "I don't like being alone, either. But there are worse things. A bad marriage is one of them."

"OK." Bob said. "Enough for now. I'll put on my smiling mask for Halloween and do the remote. But you know what would really make me happy?"

"What?"

"If we both would take our masks off and be totally honest about how we feel about each other."

"Bob, I don't know how I feel."

"I can wait." Bob smiled. "But let's see if we can put the masks away after Halloween."

On All-Hallows' Eve Bob arrived at Club 242 slightly before 6:00 P.M., the time he normally began his nightly shift. Ken Bradley was filling in at the studio until eight o'clock, then Bob was scheduled to begin the remote. Equipment was already in place down center on stage, and Bob began giving everything a final check. Live acts often played here, but this was Bob Martin night. Bob had dubbed all his numbers on long-playing cassette, which he could stop and start to allow his comments and commercials. His music also would be interspersed with various features—occasional interviews, drawings for door prizes, awards to the scariest costume, most beautiful costume, funniest costume, most creative costume, best matching his-and-her costumes.

Ralph Blakemore, the club's owner, patted him on the back.

"I like your costume. Dracula?"

"You have to ask?" Bob said, suddenly pushing something into his mouth.

"The fangs do wonders for you." Ralph nodded.

"They don't help my talking, though. I won't be able to wear them."

"You're still scary enough to keep everyone away. And if you're not, we'll have two guys this year who'll make sure nobody bothers you. Anything else you need, let me know."

"Thanks," Bob said. "How about building a closer restroom?"

Ralph smiled and walked away. The restrooms
were off the main floor, up a short flight of stairs on
the west side of the room and down a hallway that
should have been wider to accommodate the crowds
that came to the club. After checking the equipment,
Bob made sure his commercials were in proper order.
Some were recorded, but many he would give "live."
Four speakers would carry his music and comments
to the crowd while being broadcast.

The place was already crowded fifteen minutes before eight, when Penny made her appearance. She
was dressed as Tinker Bell, and the short skirt allowed Bob to admire the way her long legs filled out
the shiny green material that ended with brown san-
dals curling up at the toes. She also wore a green tu-
nic and on her head a brown cap with a long feather
pointed toward the rear. A shoulder strap supported a
bag with her portable recording equipment.

"I wish you were in costume," she said drily.

"I wish you were out of yours."

She stared at him. "Dracula wouldn't talk like
that."

"That's not Dracula talking. After this is over, Tinker Bell, will you take me to Never-Never Land?"

"Never."

"OK. Then how about coffee at Guido's?"

"If you get rid of the fangs. See you later."

He watched her move off and then made phone
contact with Ken at the studio.

The remote began promptly at eight and all went
smoothly, the noise and tempo picking up steadily as
the clock moved toward midnight. Several times he
caught a glimpse of Penny moving through the crowd
and taping conversations. Once she came close to the

stage and winked at him. His only extended relief from the mike were the hourly five-minute news-breaks, which Ralph read from the studio.

"One hour to go," he thought, standing and stretching at the eleven o'clock break. He decided to visit the restroom. Making his way up the stairs and into the hallway he thought again how old this place was. He was almost to the door of the restroom when he heard a voice yell "Fire!" Everyone in the hallway froze. He smelled smoke. Then someone screamed, joined by other shouts. People in the hallway moved toward the exit at the far end. Bob was pushed with them until the mass backed up at the door.

"It's locked!" someone yelled. Then the crowd lurched in the other direction toward the ballroom. Bob went with them, hardly able to breathe. The person ahead of him staggered at the stairs, and Bob grabbed his arm. The smoke was heavier. He fought his way over to his equipment. He gripped the mike. "Everyone please keep calm." His words blaring from the speakers were indistinguishable from the general melee. Someone fell into his table as a large group stampeded toward the exit at the rear of the stage. Now Bob could see flames licking their way up the wall to his right, and then more flames on the wall near the stairs to the restrooms. Suddenly he felt a surging fear. Where was Penny? He yelled her name. Panic was everywhere, added to his own fear for her. He pushed through the crowd shouting her name over and over. It was no use. Maybe she was all right. Maybe she had got out. But the fear tightened its grip on his heart.

Now the smoke was burning his eyes. He had to get out himself. But where was Penny? He was

coughing when he felt someone touch his shoulder.
He looked behind him and saw a man motioning him
toward the hallway stairs. Bob stared and the man
gestured again. Bob followed him. By this time the
stairs were almost empty as the flames and smoke
seemed to feed on each other. But the man still went
ahead of him. *He doesn't know the exit is locked,* Bob
thought. He tried to catch the man but lost sight of
him in the smoke. Bob yelled at him to come back,
following him deeper into the hallway. Then he saw
the man pointing to the door to the women's restroom. Bob's eyes were tearing from the smoke. He
squinted and blinked and lost sight of the man again,
but he pushed his way into the restroom. He saw
her—Penny—stretched out on the floor beneath a
lavatory. He rushed to her, picking her up. She was
breathing. He carried her into the hallway. The man
was gone. In the ballroom only a few people were
left pushing to get out the front and stage exits. Holding her tightly while coughing and stumbling, Bob
made his way out the front. Fire engines were arriv-
ing amid police sirens and flashing lights.

Bob placed Penny on the ground. A fireman rushed
to them and placed an oxygen mask over Penny's
face. After a few moments she began to stir. Her eyes
opened and then looked past the fireman at Bob
bending over anxiously. The fireman removed the
mask, and Penny smiled. "Are we still going to
Guido's?" she asked.

Later at her apartment she told Bob that she had
been washing her hands when people panicked and
someone knocked her over and she hit her head on
the lavatory. But how did he know where she was?

He told her of the man who had led him to her. But

then he told her of something else. The story of a rainy day eleven years earlier when a mentally disturbed man spoke of seeing a man with a sword. Bob hadn't believed in guardian angels. He never would unless he could see one himself. But he had seen someone at Club 242.

"He was a man," Penny said.

Bob shook his head. "I don't think so."

"You think he's your guardian angel? Then why rescue me?"

"Maybe he protects me, and those—" Bob hesitated, staring into her eyes, "—those I love."

Her eyes softened in the silence, and then she suddenly laughed. "I've got an idea."

"What?"

"Why don't I do a show on angel visits? We'll ask anyone who thinks he has seen an angel to phone and share his experience."

"You'll get a lot of kooks."

"That's where you come in."

"'What do you mean?"

"You'll be my special guest, tell your story and establish this as a legitimate and serious subject."

"They'll think *I'm* a kook."

"Maybe they'll think you're *my* kook." She put her hand behind his neck and drew him closer until their lips touched. Bob had no more doubts then. He knew he had a guardian angel.

Amazing and Inspiring True Stories of Divine Intervention

ANGELS
   by Hope Price   0-380-72331-X/$5.99 US

ANGELS AMONG US
   by Don Fearheiley
                          0-380-77377-5/$6.99 US/$9.99 Can

HOW TO TALK WITH YOUR ANGELS
   by Kim O'Neill
                          0-380-78194-8/$5.99 US/$7.99 Can